Conversation Phrase-Books

I Speak ITALIAN

CONVERSATION PHRASE-BOOK WITH PRONUNCIATION GUIDE

Rosa Anna Rizzo

A.VALLARDI

Antonio Vallardi Editore s.r.l.
Corso Italia 13 - 20122 Milano

Ristampe: 10 9 8 7
2003 2002

ISBN 88-8211-165-2

CONTENTS

i PRONUNCIATION AND PHONETIC TRANSCRIPTION

GUIDE TO PRONUNCIATION

You'll find the pronunciation of the Italian letters and sounds explained below, as well as the symbols we're using for them in the transcriptions.
The imitated pronunciation should be read as if it were English.

The Italian language possesses twenty-two letters, of which *a, e, i, o, u* are vowels; the others are consonants.
The Italian alphabet

a	*ah*	n	*ennay*
b	*bee*	o	*oh*
c	*chee*	p	*pee*
d	*dee*	q	*koo*
e	*ay*	r	*erray*
f	*effay*	s	*essay*
g	*gee*	t	*tee*
h	*ahkkah*	u	*oo*
i	*ee*	v	*vee*
j	*ee loonggoh*	z	*zaytah*
l	*ellay*		
m	*emmay*		

The letters *k, w, x, y* do not exist in Italian.

Pronunciation of vowels

a is sounded broad like the *a* in rather *ah*
Example: lana [*lahnah*]

e can always be pronounced like *ay* in way
Example: fede [*fayday*]

i is pronounced like the English *ee* in sleep
Example: finire [*feeneeray*]

o can always be pronounced *o* as in got
Example: nota [*nohtah*]

u is pronounced like *oo* in moon
Example: luna [*loonah*]
In diphthongs each vowel must be pronounced separately
Example: buono [*booohnoh*]

Pronunciation of consonants

The consonants *b, d, f, l, m, n, p, t, v,* are always pronounced as in English.

c	before *a, e, u* and before consonants is pronounced like *k* in cat Example: cosa [*kohsah*]
c	before *e, i* sounds as in the English *cha* in chase, *chee* in cheese Example: cena [*chaynah*]
g	before *a, o, u* is pronounced hard like the English god Example: galante [*gahlahntay*]
g	before *e, i* is pronounced like *j* in jet Example: gentile [*jenteelay*]
gg	before *e, i* is pronounced like *dg* in badge Example: coraggio [*kohrahdjoh*]
ghe, ghi	sound as in guess, guilt Example: ghiaccio [*gheeahchchoh*]
gl	followed by *a, e, o, u* is pronounced like *gl* in gland Example: gloria [*glohreeah*]
gli	sounds like *lli* in brilliant Example: egli [*aylyee*]
gn	is pronounced more like the *ni* in opinion Example: campagna [*kahmpahnyah*]
h	is never pronounced
q	which is always followed by *u*, is pronounced as in question Example: questo [*kwesstoh*]
r	must be very distinctly pronounced
s	generally like *s* in sit, sometimes like *z* in zoo Example: servo [*sehrvoh*]; viso [*veezoh*]
sce, sci	sound like *sh* in shell Example: uscita [*oosheetah*]
z, zz	sounds generally like *ts* in hits, sometimes like *ds* in roads Example: grazie [*grahtseeay*]; canzone [*kahntzohnay*]

Stressing of words

Generally, the vowel of the next to last syllable is stressed.
When a final vowel is stressed, it has an accent written over it (andò).
Normally an accent is used only when the stress falls on a final vowel.

USEFUL ADJECTIVES

able	capace [*kahpahchay*]
unable	incapace [*eenkahpahchay*]
amusing	divertente [*deevehrtentay*]
boring	noioso [*nohyohzoh*]
beautiful	bello [*belloh*]
ugly	brutto [*broottoh*]
best	migliore [*meelyoray*]
worst	peggiore [*paydjohray*]
big	grande [*grahnday*]
little	piccolo [*peekkohloh*]
clean	pulito [*pooleetoh*]
dirty	sporco [*sporkoh*]
cultured	colto [*kolltoh*]
ignorant	ignorante [*eenyohrahntay*]
deep	profondo [*prohfondoh*]
shallow	superficiale [*soopehrfeechyahlay*]
dry	secco [*seckkoh*]
damp	umido [*oomeedoh*]
dry	asciutto [*ahshoottoh*]
wet	bagnato [*bahnyahtoh*]
easy	facile [*fahcheelay*]
difficult	difficile [*deefeecheelay*]
expensive	caro [*kahroh*]
cheap	a buon mercato [*ah booohn mayrkahtoh*]
fair-blond	biondo [*beeondoh*]
dark (haired)	bruno [*broonoh*]
famous	famoso [*fahmohzoh*]
unknown	sconosciuto [*skonossshootoh*]
fast	veloce [*vaylohchay*]
slow	lento [*lentoh*]
fat	grasso [*grahssoh*]
thin	magro [*mahgroh*]
fragile	fragile [*frahjeelay*]
unbreakable	infrangibile [*eenfrahnjeebeelay*]
free, vacant	libero [*leebayroh*]
engaged, occupied	occupato [*okkoopahtoh*]
fresh	fresco [*frayskoh*]
tired	stanco [*stahnkoh*]
generous	generoso [*jaynayrohzoh*]
greedy	avaro [*ahvahroh*]
good	buono [*booohnoh*]
bad	cattivo [*kahtteevoh*]
hard	duro [*dooroh*]
soft	molle [*mollay*]
healthy, well	sano [*sahnoh*]

ill	malato [*mahlahtoh*]
high	alto [*ahltoh*]
low	basso [*bahssoh*]
hot	caldo [*kahldoh*]
cold	freddo [*freddoh*]
important	importante [*eemportahntay*]
unimportant	non importante [*nonn eemportahntay*]
intelligent	intelligente [*eentelleejentay*]
stupid	stupido [*stoopeedoh*]
kind	gentile [*jenteelay*]
rude	sgarbato [*sgahrbahtoh*]
light (colour)	chiaro [*keeahroh*]
dark (colour)	scuro [*skooroh*]
light (weight)	leggero [*laydjayroh*]
heavy	pesante [*paysahntay*]
long	lungo [*loongoh*]
short	corto [*korrtoh*]
merry	allegro [*ahllaygroh*]
sad	triste [*treestay*]
necessary	necessario [*naychessahreeoh*]
extra, superfluous	superfluo [*soopehrflooh*]
new	nuovo [*nooohvoh*]
second-hand, used	usato [*oozahtoh*]
nice	simpatico [*seempahteekoh*]
nasty	antipatico [*ahnteepahteekoh*]
open	aperto [*ahpehrtoh*]
shut	chiuso [*keeoosoh*]
pleasant	piacevole [*peeahchayvohlay*]
unpleasant	spiacevole [*speeahchayvohlay*]
public	pubblico [*poobbleekoh*]
private	privato [*preevahtoh*]
rich	ricco [*reekkoh*]
poor	povero [*pohvayroh*]
straight	diritto [*dreettoh*]
crooked	storto [*stortoh*]
strong	forte [*fortay*]
weak	debole [*daybohlay*]
sweet	dolce [*dollchay*]
bitter	amaro [*ahmahroh*]
tall	alto [*ahltoh*]
short	basso [*bahssoh*]
useful	utile [*ooteelay*]
useless	inutile [*eenooteelay*]
wide	largo [*lahrgoh*]
narrow	stretto [*strettoh*]
young	giovane [*johvahnay*]
old	vecchio [*veckkeeoh*]

COLOURS

black	nero [*nayroh*]
blue	blu [*bloo*]

brown	marrone [*mahrrohnay*]
gray	grigio [*greejoh*]
green	verde [*vehrday*]
mauve	lilla [*leellah*]
orange	arancione [*ahrahnchohnay*]
pale blue	celeste [*chaylesstay*]
pink	rosa [*rohzah*]
purple	viola [*veeohla*]
red	rosso [*rossoh*]
sky blue	azzurro [*ahtzoorroh*]
white	bianco [*beeahngkoh*]
yellow	giallo [*jahlloh*]

COMMON PHRASES

Best wishes	Tanti auguri, tanti saluti [*tahntee owgooree, tahntee sahlootee*]
By the way	A proposito [*ah prohpohzeetoh*]
Come here!	Venite qua! [*vayneetay kwah*]
Come in	Avanti [*ahvahntee*]
Congratulations!	Congratulazioni! [*congrahtoolahtzeeohnee!*] Felicitazioni! [*fayleecheetahtzeeohnee!*] Rallegramenti! [*rahllaygrahmentee!*]
Could you do me a favour?	Potete farmi un favore? [*pohtaytay fahrmee oon fahvoray?*]
Do you mind my smoking?	Permette che fumi? [*pehrmettay kay foomee?*]
Do you smoke?	Lei fuma? [*layee foomah?*]
Do you speak English?	Parla inglese? [*pahrlah eenglayzay?*]
Don't mention it, its a pleasure	Prego [*praygoh*]
Don't talk nonsense!	Non dire sciocchezze! [*non deeray shockketsay*]
Excuse me!	Scusate! [*skoozahtay*] Scusi [*skoozee*]
Excuse me, what did you say?	Scusate, come avete detto? [*skoozahtay, kommay ahvaytay dettoh?*]
Fancy that! Just fancy!	Figuratevi [*feegoorahtayvee*]
Go away!	Vattene! [*vahtaynay!*]
Good-bye!	Addio! [*ahddeeoh!*]
Good evening	Buona sera [*booohnah sayrah*]
Good luck!	Buona fortuna! [*booohnah fortoonah*]
Good morning, sir/madam/miss	Buon giorno, signore [*booohn jorrnoh seenyoray*] signora [*seenyorah*] signorina [*seenyoreenah*]
Good-night	Buona notte [*booohnah nottay*]
Help!	Aiuto! [*aheeyootoh*]
How are you?	Come state? [*kommay stahtay?*]
Not at all well	Male [*mahlay*]
Not very well	Non molto bene [*non molltoh baynay*]
Very well, thank you	Benissimo, grazie [*bayneesseemoh, grahtzeeay*]
Hurry up!	Spicciati! [*speechahtee*]
I am afraid that...	Temo che... [*taymoh kay...*]
I am glad	Mi fa piacere [*mee fah pyahchayray*]
I am sorry	Mi dispiace [*mee deespeeahchay*]
I am sure that...	Sono sicuro che... [*sohnoh seekooroh kay*]
I cannot	Non posso [*non posssoh*]
I don't doubt that...	Non dubito che... [*non doobeetoh kay...*]

I don't know	Non lo so [*non loh soh*]
I don't understand you	Non vi capisco [*non vee kahpeeskoh*]
I feel ill	Mi sento male [*mee sentoh mahlay*]
I suppose that...	Suppongo che... [*sooppongoh kay...*]
I won't fail	Non mancherò [*non mahnkayro*]
It doesn't matter	Non importa [*nonn eemportah*]
It isn't worth it	Non vale la pena [*non vahlay lah paynah*]
Just imagine that...	Figurati che... [*feegooruhtee kay...*]
Leave me in peace! **Let me alone!**	Lasciami in pace! [*lahshahmee een pahchay*]
Lucky thing! (him)	Beato lui [*bayahtoh looee*]
May I come in? **May I get past?**	Permesso [*pehrmesssoh*]
My compliments!	Complimenti [*kompleementee*]
My name is...	Mi chiamo... [*mee kyahmoh...*]
My regards, my respects	I miei ossequi [*ee meeayee ohsaykwee*]
Please	Per piacere [*pehr peeahchayray*] Per favore [*pehr fahvoray*]
Please speak slowly	Parli adagio, per favore [*pahrlee ahdahjyoh, pehr fahvoray*]
Serve him right!	Peggio per lui [*payjyoh pehr looee*]
Shame!	Che vergogna! [*kay vayrgonyah*]
Shut up!	Taci [*tahchee*]
Stop it!	Smettila! [*smaytteelah*]
Thank you	Grazie [*grahtzeeay*]
Wait a minute	Aspettate un momento [*ahspettahtay oon mohmentoh*]
What a lovely surprise!	Che bella sorpresa! [*kay bellah sorprayzah*]
What a pity!	Che peccato! [*kay paykkahtoh*]
What bad luck!	Che sfortuna! [*kay sfortoonah*]
What do you want?	Che cosa volete? [*kay kohsah volaytay?*]
What does that mean?	Che cosa vuol dire? [*kay kohsah vooohl deeray?*]
What is the matter?	Che cosa c'è? [*kay kohsah chay?*]
What is the time?	Che ore sono? [*kay oray sohnoh?*]
What is your name?	Come vi chiamate? [*kommay vee kyahmahtay?*]
Where are you going?	Dove andate? [*dohvay ahndahtay?*]
Where do you come from?	Da dove venite? [*dah dohvay vayneetay*]
Where is the...?	Dov'è il...? [*dohvay eel...?*]
With pleasure, gladly	Volontieri [*vollonteeayree*]
You are a brick	Sei un tesoro [*sayee oon tayzoroh*]
You are mistaken	Ti sbagli [*tee sbahlyee*]
You are right	Hai ragione [*ahee rahjyohnay*]
You are wrong	Hai torto [*ahee tortoh*]

(to) accept an invitation	accettare un invito [*ahchchettahray oon eenveetoh*]
(to) appreciate	gradire [*grahdeeray*]
appreciated	gradito [*grahdeetoh*]
(to) be introduced	essere presentato [*esssayray prayzentahtoh*]
(to) be late	essere in ritardo [*esssayray een reetahrdoh*]
(to) be on time	essere puntuale [*esssayray poontooahlay*]
bunch of flowers	mazzo di fiori [*mahtzoh dee feeohree*]
conversation	conversazione [*konvehrsahtseeohnay*]
(to) decline an invitation	rifiutare un invito [*reefyootahray oon eenveetoh*]
dining-room	sala da pranzo [*sahlah dah prahntsoh*]
flowers	fiori [*feeohree*]
friend	amico/amica [*ahmeekoh/ahmeekah*]
friendship	amicizia [*ahmeecheetseeah*]
gentleman	signore [*seenyohray*]
gentlemen	signori [*seenyohree*]
(to) give hospitality	ospitare [*osspeetahray*]
(to) greet	salutare [*sahlootahray*]
greetings	saluti [*sahlootee*]
guest	ospite [*osspeetay*]
high life	vita di società [*veetah dee sohcheeaytah*]
hospitality	ospitalità [*osspeetahleetah*]
host	padrone di casa [*pahdrohnay dee kahsah*]
hostess	padrona di casa [*pahdrohnah dee kahsah*]
house, home	casa [*kahsah*]
(to) introduce oneself	presentarsi [*prayzentahrsee*]
introduction	presentazione [*prayzentahtseeohnay*]
invitation	invito [*eenveetoh*]
(to) invite	invitare [*eenveetahray*]
kind	gentile [*jenteelay*]
kindness	gentilezza [*jenteeletzah*]
(to) know	conoscere [*kohnohshayray*]
lady	signora [*seenyohrah*]
(to) leave somebody in the lurch	piantare in asso qualcuno [*peeahntahray een ahssoh kwahlkoonoh*]
(to) make an appointment	prendere un appuntamento [*prendayray oon ahppoontahmentoh*]
(to) make friends with	fare amicizia con [*fahray ahmeecheetseeah kon*]
(to) make the acquaintance of	fare la conoscenza di [*fahray lah kohnohshentzah dee*]
(to) miss an appointment	mancare all'appuntamento [*mahnkahray ahllahppoontahmentoh*]
Miss Brown	signorina Brown [*seenyohreenah Brown*]
Mr. Brown	signor Brown [*seenyohr Brown*]

(to) pay a visit	fare una visita [*fahray oonah veezeetah*]
pleasure	piacere [*peeahchayray*]
polite	cortese [*korrtayzay*]
politeness	cortesia [*korrtayzeeah*]
(to) receive	accogliere [*ahkkohlyayray*]
(to) receive an invitation	ricevere un invito [*reechayvayray oon eenveetoh*]
reception	ricevimento [*reechayveementoh*]
sitting-room	salotto [*sahlottoh*]
(to) speak	parlare [*pahrlahray*]
society	società [*sohcheeaytah*]
subject of conversation	argomento di conversazione [*ahrgohmentoh dee konvehrsahtseeohnay*]
(to) talk	conversare [*konvehrsahray*]
(to) telephone	telefonare [*taylayfohnahray*]
(to) thank	ringraziare [*reengrahtseeahray*]
(to) trouble	disturbare [*deestoorbahray*]
trouble	disturbo [*deestoorboh*]
visit	visita [*veezeetah*]
visiting-card	biglietto da visita [*beelyettoh dah veezeetah*]
young lady	signorina [*seenyohreenah*]

GREETINGS AND INTRODUCTIONS

> Remember that familiar forms are only used when you know someone well or are invited to do so. Otherwise use the formal forms.

good morning/good afternoon	buon giorno [*booohn jorrnoh*], literally good day, used like the English good morning, but also in the early afternoon
good evening	buona sera [*booohnah sayrah*], used in the late afternoon and in the evening
good night	buona notte [*booohnah nohttay*]
hello/hi there	ciao [*chaoh*], a casual greeting used among friends
goodbye	arrivederci [*ahrreevaydayrchee*]
see you later	a più tardi [*ah peeoo tahrdee*]
see you soon	a presto [*ah presstoh*]
This is Mr./Mrs./Miss...	Le presento il signor/la signora/la signorina [*lay prayzentoh eel seenyohr/lah seenyohrah/lah seenyohreenah*]
How do you do?	Piacere! [*peeahchayray*]
Pleased to meet you	Molto lieto [*mohltoh leeaytoh*]
How are you?	Come sta? [*kohmay stah*]

Very well, thanks. And you?	Molto bene, grazie. E lei? [*mohltoh baynay, grahtseeay. Ay layee*]
How's life?	Come va? [*kohmay vah*]
Fine	Bene [*baynay*]

CALLING ON

Please, will you take a seat?	Prego, si accomodi [*praygoh, see ahkkohmohdee*]
I'm glad to see you	Sono lieto di vederla [*sohnoh leeaytoh dee vaydayrlah*]
May I offer you a cup of tea?	Posso offrirle una tazza di tè [*pohssoh offreerlay oonah tahtsah dee tay*]
Would you like some milk or lemon in your tea? Sugar?	Vuole latte o limone nel tè? Zucchero? [*vooohlay lahttay oh leemohnay nell tay? tsookkayroh*]
What will you have? A glass of... a soft drink?	Cosa prende: un bicchiere di... una bibita? [*kohsah prenday: oon beekkeeayray dee... oonah beebeetah*]
Nothing, thank you	Niente, grazie [*neeentay, grahtseeay*]
Now I must be going	Ora devo andare [*ohrah dayvoh ahndahray*]
It has been a very pleasant evening	È stata una piacevole serata [*ay stahtah oonah peeahchayvohlay sayrahtah*]
Thank you for all your kindness	Grazie per la sua cortese ospitalità [*grahtseeay pehr lah sooah korrtayzay osspeetahleetah*]
Let's hope to meet again soon	Speriamo di rivederci presto [*spayreeahmoh dee reevaydehrchee presstoh*]
Next time we expect you at our home	La prossima volta vi aspettiamo a casa nostra [*lah prossseemah volltah vee ahspetteeahmoh ah kahsah nosstrah*]
With pleasure	Volentieri [*vohlenteeayree*]
My turn next time!	A buon rendere! [*ah booohn rendayray*]
Would you like to have dinner with us on...?	Vorrebbe cenare con noi il... [*vorraybbay chaynahray kon nohee eel...*]
I am sorry, but I already have an engagement	Spiacente ma ho già un impegno [*speeahchentay mah oh jah oon eempaynyoh*]

WISHES

Best wishes	Tanti auguri [*tahntee owgooree*]
Congratulations	Rallegramenti [*rahllaygrahmentee*]
Good luck/all the best	Buona fortuna [*booohnah forrtoonah*]
Have a nice trip!	Buon viaggio! [*booohn veeahdjoh*]
Have a good holiday!	Buone vacanze! [*booohnay vahkahntsay*]

Enjoy yourself, have a good time!	Divertiti! [*deevehrteetee*]
Happy birthday!	Buon compleanno! [*booohn komplayahnnoh*]
Many happy returns!	Cento di questi giorni! [*chentoh dee qwesstee jorrnee*]
Merry Christmas!	Buon Natale! [*booohn nahtahlay*]
Happy New Year!	Felice anno nuovo! [*fayleechay ahnnoh nooohvoh*]
Happy Easter!	Buona Pasqua! [*booohnah pahskwah*]

iii NUMBERS, WEIGHTS AND MEASURES

NUMBERS

CARDINAL NUMBERS

1	uno	[*oonoh*]
2	due	[*dooay*]
3	tre	[*tray*]
4	quattro	[*kwahttroh*]
5	cinque	[*cheenkway*]
6	sei	[*sayee*]
7	sette	[*settay*]
8	otto	[*ottoh*]
9	nove	[*nohvay*]
10	dieci	[*deeaychee*]
11	undici	[*oondeechee*]
12	dodici	[*dohdeechee*]
13	tredici	[*traydeechee*]
14	quattordici	[*kwahttordeechee*]
15	quindici	[*kweendeechee*]
16	sedici	[*saydeechee*]
17	diciassette	[*deechahssettay*]
18	diciotto	[*deechottoh*]
19	diciannove	[*deechahnnohvay*]
20	venti	[*ventee*]
21	ventuno	[*ventoonoh*]
22	ventidue	[*venteedooay*]
23	ventitre	[*venteetray*]
30	trenta	[*trentah*]
31	trentuno	[*trentoonoh*]
40	quaranta	[*kwahrahntah*]
41	quarantuno	[*kwahranhtoonoh*]
50	cinquanta	[*cheenkwahntah*]
51	cinquantuno	[*cheenkwahntoonoh*]
60	sessanta	[*sayssahntah*]
61	sessantuno	[*sayssahntoonoh*]
70	settanta	[*sayttahntah*]
71	settantuno	[*sayttahntoonoh*]
80	ottanta	[*ottahntah*]
81	ottantuno	[*ottahntoonoh*]
90	novanta	[*nohvahntah*]
91	novantuno	[*nohvahntoonoh*]
100	cento	[*chentoh*]
101	centouno	[*chentohoonoh*]
200	duecento	[*dooaychentoh*]
1 000	mille	[*meellay*]
10 000	diecimila	[*deeaycheemeelah*]
100 000	centomila	[*chentohmeelah*]
1 000 000	un milione	[*oon meeleeohnay*]

1st	primo	[*preemoh*]
2nd	secondo	[*saykondoh*]
3rd	terzo	[*tehrtsoh*]
4th	quarto	[*kwahrtoh*]
5th	quinto	[*kweentoh*]
6th	sesto	[*sesstoh*]
7th	settimo	[*setteemoh*]
8th	ottavo	[*ottahvoh*]
9th	nono	[*nonoh*]
10th	decimo	[*daycheemoh*]
11th	undicesimo	[*oondeechayzeemoh*]
12th	dodicesimo	[*dohdeechayzeemoh*]
13th	tredicesimo	[*traydeechayzeemoh*]
20th	ventesimo	[*ventayzeemoh*]
21st	ventunesimo	[*ventoonayzeemoh*]
30th	trentesimo	[*trentayzeemoh*]
100th	centesimo	[*chentayzeemoh*]
1000th	millesimo	[*meellayzeemoh*]

WEIGHTS AND MEASURES

A matter which is likely to cause some confusion when reading figures is that the decimal point in Italian is indicated by a comma on the line: thus 103.6 is written 103,6.
On the other hand, a point, and not a comma is used after every third number in a large figure: thus 4.566 indicates four thousand, five hundred and sixty-six.

WEIGHT

1	grain	0,065	g
1	drachm	1,77	g
1	ounce (oz)	28,35	g
1	pound (1b) = 16 oz	453,6	g
1	stone = 14 1b	6,35	kg
1	hundredweight (cwt) = 112 1b	50,8	kg
1	ton = 20 cwt	1,016	tonne
		(1,120	U.S. short ton)

LIQUID MEASURE

1	minim	0,059	ml
1	fluid drachm	3,55	ml
1	fluid ounce (vol. of 1 oz water)	28,4	ml
1	Imperial pint (pt) = 20 fl oz	568	ml
1	Imperial quart (qt) = 2 pt	1,14	l
1	Imperial gallon = 8 pt	4,55	l
		(1,201	U.S. gal.)

LENGTH

1	inch (in)	2,54	cm
1	foot (ft) = 12 in	0,305	m
1	yard (yd) = 3 ft	0,9144	m
1	mile = 1760 yd	1,61	km
1	nautical mile (6080 ft)	1,85	km

iV TIME AND WEATHER

TIME

The 24-hour clock is used widely, thus, you may hear:

le ore ventidue [*lay ohray venteedooay*]	22.00	10.00	pm
le quindici meno dieci [*lay kweendeechee maynoh deeaychee*]	14.50	2.50	pm

What time is it?	Che ora è/Che ore sono? [*kay ohrah ay/kay ohray sohnoh*]
It's...	È/Sono... [*ay/sohnoh*]
6.00	le sei [*lay sayee*]
6.05	le sei e cinque [*lay sayee ay cheenkway*]
6.10	le sei e dieci [*lay sayee ay deeaychee*]
6.15	le sei e un quarto [*lay sayee ay oon kwahrtoh*]
6.20	le sei e venti [*lay sayee ay ventee*]
6.25	le sei e venticinque [*lay sayee ay venteecheenkway*]
6.30	le sei e mezza [*lay sayee ay medzah*]
6.35	le sei e trentacinque [*lay sayee ay trentah cheenkway*]
6.40	le sette meno venti [*lay settay maynoh ventee*]
6.45	le sette meno un quarto [*lay settay maynoh oon kwahrtoh*]
6.50	le sette meno dieci [*lay settah maynoh deeaychee*]
6.55	le sette meno cinque [*lay settay maynoh cheenkway*]
midday	mezzogiorno [*medzohjorrnoh*]
midnight	mezzanotte [*medzahnottay*]
in the morning	del mattino [*dayl mahtteenoh*]
in the afternoon	del pomeriggio [*dayl pohmayreedjoh*]
in the evening	della sera [*dayllah sayrah*]
When does the train leave?	A che ora parte il treno? [*ah kay ohrah pahrtay eel traynoh?*]
The train is due at 5.00 pm sharp	Il treno arriva alle 17 in punto [*eel traynoh ahrreevah ahllay deechahssettay een poontoh*]
The coach leaves every quarter of an hour; every half hour; every twenty minutes; every two hours	La corriera parte ogni quarto d'ora, ogni mezz'ora, ogni venti minuti, ogni due ore [*lah korrreeayrah pahrtay ohnyee kwahrtoh dohrah, ohnyee medzzohrah, ohnyee ventee meenootee; ohnyee dooay ohray*]

It is late	È tardi [*ay tahrdee*]
It is early	È presto [*ay presstoh*]
What time do you open?	A che ora apre? [*ah kay ohrah ahpray*]
How long will it take to get there?	Quanto ci vorrà per arrivarci? [*kwantoh chee vohrrah pehr ahrreevahrchee*]
We can be there in less than half an hour	Possiamo arrivarci in meno di mezz'ora [*possseeahmoh ahrreevahrchee een maynoh dee medzzohrah*]
We'll be back very late	Torneremo molto tardi [*tohrnayraymoh mohltoh tahrdee*]
The clock is fast/slow	L'orologio è avanti/indietro [*lohrohlohjoh ay ahvahntee/eendeeaytroh*]

DAYS AND DATE

What's the date today?	Quanti ne abbiamo oggi? [*kwantee nay ahbbeeahmoh odjee*]
It's the Ist of May	È il primo maggio [*ay eel preemoh madjoh*]
2nd of March	Il due marzo [*eel dooay mahrtzoh*]
Sunday	domenica [*dohmayneekah*]
Monday	lunedì [*loonaydee*]
Tuesday	martedì [*mahrtaydee*]
Wednesday	mercoledì [*mehrkohlaydee*]
Thursday	giovedì [*johvaydee*]
Friday	venerdì [*vaynehrdee*]
Saturday	sabato [*sahbahtoh*]
The day before yesterday	ieri l'altro [*eeayree lahltroh*]
yesterday	ieri [*eeayree*]
today	oggi [*odjee*]
tomorrow	domani [*dohmahnee*]
the day after tomorrow	dopodomani [*dohpohdohmahnee*]
the next day	il giorno seguente [*eel jorrnoh saygwayntay*]
some days ago	alcuni giorni fa [*ahlkoonee jorrnee fah*]
last month	il mese scorso [*eel maysay skohrsoh*]
next week	la settimana prossima [*lah setteemahnah prossseemah*]
working days	giorni feriali [*jorrnee fayreeahlee*]

HOLIDAYS

Most Italians take their holidays in August, so Ferragosto, 15 August, is one of the most important public holidays and many towns hold fireworks displays to celebrate it. The sign "Chiuso per ferie" on a shop or restaurant door or window means "Closed for the holidays".

New Year's Eve (December 31st)	San Silvestro [*sahn Seelvesstroh*]
New Year's Day (January 1st)	Capodanno [*kahpohdahnnoh*]
Easter (movable date)	Pasqua [*pahskwah*]
Epiphany (January 6th)	Epifania [*aypeefahneeah*]
Liberation Day (April 25th)	Anniversario della liberazione (1945) [*ahneevehrsahreeoh delllah leebayrahtseeohnay*]
Labour Day (May 1st)	Festa del lavoro [*fesstah dell lahvohroh*]
Assumption Day (August 15th)	Ferragosto [*fehrrahgohstoh*]
All Saints' Day (November 1st)	Ognissanti [*ohnyeesahntee*]
Immaculate Conception (December 8th)	Immacolata Concezione [*eemmahkohlahtah kohnchaytseeohnay*]
Christmas Day (December 25th)	Natale [*nahtahlay*]
St. Stephen's Day (December 26th)	Santo Stefano [*sahntoh stayfahnoh*]

MONTHS OF THE YEAR

January	gennaio [*jennahyoh*]
February	febbraio [*febbrahyoh*]
March	marzo [*mahrtzoh*]
April	aprile [*ahpreelay*]
May	maggio [*mahdjoh*]
June	giugno [*joonyoh*]
July	luglio [*loolyoh*]
August	agosto [*ahgosstoh*]
September	settembre [*settembray*]
October	ottobre [*ottohbray*]
November	novembre [*nohvembray*]
December	dicembre [*deechembray*]

THE SEASONS

spring	primavera [*preemahvayrah*]
summer	estate [*esstahtay*]
autumn (fall)	autunno [*awtoonnoh*]
winter	inverno [*eenvehrnoh*]
high season	alta stagione [*ahltah stahjohnay*]
low season	bassa stagione [*bahssah stahjohnay*]
wintry season	stagione invernale [*stahjohnay eenvehrnahlay*]

TELLING THE AGE

How old are you?	Quanti anni ha/hai? [*kwahntee ahnnee ah/ahee?*]
I'm 20 years old	Ho vent'anni [*oh ventahnnee*]
When were you born?	Quando sei nato? [*kwahndoh sayee nahtoh?*]
I was born in 1970	Sono nato nel 1970 [*sohnoh nahtoh nayl meellaynohvaychayntohsettahntah*]
Children under 14 are not admitted	Vietato ai minori di 14 anni [*veeaytahtoh ahee meenohree dee kwahttorrdeechee ahnnee*]
under age	minorenne [*meenohrennay*]
of age	maggiorenne [*mahdjdjohrennay*]

WEATHER

air	aria [*ahreeah*]
climate	clima [*kleemah*]
cloud	nuvola [*noovohlah*]
cloudy	nuvoloso [*noovohlohzoh*]
cold	freddo [*freddoh*]
damp	umido [*oomeedoh*]
dry	secco [*seckkoh*]
fog	nebbia [*nebbeeah*]
foggy	nebbioso [*nebbeeohsoh*]
(to) freeze	gelare [*jaylahray*]
frozen	gelato [*jaylahtoh*]
hail	grandine [*grahndeenay*]
heat	caldo [*kahldoh*]
hot (adj)	caldo [*kahldoh*]
hurricane	uragano [*oorahgahnoh*]
ice	ghiaccio [*gheeahchchoh*]
lightning	lampo [*lahmpoh*]
mist	foschia [*fosskeeah*]
moon	luna [*loonah*]
rain	pioggia [*peeohdjah*]
rainbow	arcobaleno [*ahrkohbahlaynoh*]
shower	acquazzone [*ahkkwahtzohnay*]
sky	cielo [*chayloh*]
snow	neve [*nayvay*]
star	stella [*stelllah*]
storm	temporale [*tempohrahlay*]
sultry	afoso [*ahfohsoh*]
sun	sole [*sohlay*]
temperature	temperatura [*taympayrahtoorah*]
thunder	tuono [*tooohnoh*]
wind	vento [*vayntoh*]

What's the weather like?	Che tempo fa? [*kay tempoh fah?*]
It's a lovely day	È una bella giornata [*ay oonah belllah jorrnahtah*]
It's sunny	C'è il sole [*chay eel sohlay*]
Is it going to rain?	Pioverà? [*peeohvayray*]
What awful weather!	Che tempo orribile! [*kay tempoh orrreebeelay!*]
What is the weather forecast?	Come sono le previsioni del tempo? [*kohmay sohnoh lay prayveezeeohnee dell tempoh?*]
Is the weather going to change?	Il tempo cambierà? [*eel tempoh kahmbeeayrah?*]
Is it going to be fine?	Sarà una bella giornata? [*sahrah oonah belllah jorrnahtah?*]
The sun is shining, the sun is burning	Il sole splende, il sole picchia [*eel sohlay splenday, eel sohlay peekkeeah*]

What is the temperature?	Quanti gradi ci sono? [*kwahntee grahdee chee sohnoh?*]
Two below zero	2 gradi sotto zero [*dooay grahdee sottoh dzayroh*]
The wind is blowing hard	Tira forte vento [*teerah fohrtay ventoh*]
There's a nice breeze blowing	C'è un bel venticello [*chay oon bell vaynteechaylloh*]
It is warm/it is cold/it is windy	Fa caldo/fa freddo/c'è vento [*fah kahldoh/fah freddoh/chay vayntoh*]
The climate is mild/harsh/dry/humid	Il clima è mite/rigido/secco/umido [*eel kleemah ay meetay/reejeedoh/seckkoh/oomeedoh*]

THE TEMPERATURE

The Centigrade system is in use in Italy.
Normal body temperature:
Fahrenheit 98.4° = Centigrade 36.7°

Fahrenheit	Centigrade
212	100
194	90
176	80
158	70
140	60
122	50
113	45
107.6	42
105.8	41
104.0	40
102.2	39
100.4	38
98.6	37
96.8	36
95	35
86	30
77	25
68	20
59	15
50	10
41	5
32	0
23	— 5
14	—10

V NOTICES AND WARNINGS

affittasi [*ahffeettahsee*]	(to) let
aperto da... a... [*ahpayrtoh dah... ah...*]	open from... to...
arrivo [*ahrreevoh*]	arrival
ascensore [*ahshensohray*]	lift
attenti al cane [*ahttentee ahl kahnay*]	beware of the dog
attenzione [*ahttentseeohnay*]	beware
avanti [*ahvahntee*]	come in!
azienda di soggiorno e turismo [*ahtseeayndah dee sohdjorrnoh ay tooreesmoh*]	tourist bureau
benvenuti [*benvaynootee*]	welcome
caldo [*kahldoh*]	hot
camera ammobiliata [*kahmayrah ahmohbeelyahtah*]	furnished room
cassa [*kahssah*]	cash desk
centro città [*chayntroh cheettah*]	city centre
chiudere la porta [*keeoodayray lah porrtah*]	close the door
chiuso [*keeoosoh*]	closed
chiuso per ferie [*keeoosoh pehr fayreeay*]	closed for holidays
chiuso per lutto [*keeoosoh pehr loottoh*]	closed: death in the family
chiuso per riposo settimanale [*keeoosoh pehr reepohsoh saytteemahnahlay*]	weekly closing day
completo [*kohmplaytoh*]	full.../no vacancies
deviazione [*dayveeahtseeohnay*]	detour
divieto di affissione [*deeveeaytoh dee ahffeesseeohnay*]	no bill-posting allowed
divieto di caccia [*deeveeaytoh dee kahchchah*]	hunting forbidden
divieto di ingresso [*deeveeaytoh dee eengresssoh*]	no entrance
divieto di scarico [*deeveeaytoh dee skahreekoh*]	no unloading
entrare senza bussare [*entrahray sentsah boossahray*]	enter without knocking
entrata libera [*entrahtah leebayrah*]	free entrance
freddo [*freddoh*]	cold
fuori servizio [*fooohree sehrveetseeoh*]	out of order
gabinetti [*gahbeenettee*]	lavatories
informazioni [*eenfohrmahtseeohnee*]	information
ingresso [*eengresssoh*]	entrance
ingresso libero [*eengresssoh leebayroh*]	entrance free
in sciopero [*een shohpayroh*]	on strike
in vendita [*een vendeetah*]	for sale

i trasgressori saranno puniti [*ee trahsgresssohree sahrahnnoh pooneetee*]	trespassers will be prosecuted
lavori in corso [*lahvohree een kohrsoh*]	work in progress
libero [*leebayroh*]	vacant
non disturbare [*nonn deestoorbahray*]	do not disturb
occupato [*ockkoopahtoh*]	occupied
orario continuato [*ohrahreoh konteenooahtoh*]	continued working hours
pagate alla cassa [*pahgahtay ahllah kahssah*]	pay at the cash desk
partenza [*pahrtentzah*]	departure
pericolo [*payreekohloh*]	danger
pista per ciclisti [*peestah pehr cheekleestee*]	path for cyclists
premere il bottone [*praymayray eel bottohnay*]	press the button
prudenza [*proodentsah*]	caution
riservato [*reesehrvahtoh*]	reserved
saldi [*sahldee*]	sales
senso unico [*saynsoh ooneekoh*]	one way
signore [*seenyohray*]	ladies (lavatory)
signori [*seenyohree*]	gentlemen (lavatory)
silenzio [*seelentseeoh*]	silence
spingere [*speenjayray*]	push
strada privata [*strahdah preevahtah*]	private road
strada senza uscita [*strahdah sentsah oosheetah*]	blind alley
suonare, per favore [*sooohnahray pehr fahvohray*]	please ring
tirare [*teerahray*]	pull
torno subito [*torrnoh soobeetoh*]	back soon
uscita [*oosheetah*]	exit
uscita di sicurezza [*oosheetah dee seekooretsah*]	emergency exit
vendita all'asta [*vendeetah ahll ahstah*]	auction sale
vernice fresca [*vayrneechay frayskah*]	wet paint
vietato [*veeaytahtoh*]	forbidden...
vietato bagnarsi [*veeaytahtoh bahnyahrsee*]	no bathing
vietato calpestare le aiuole [*veeaytahtoh kahlpaystahray lay aheeooohlay*]	keep off the grass
vietato dar cibo agli animali [*veeaytahtoh dahray cheeboh ahlyee ahneemahlee*]	please do not feed the animals
vietato fumare [*veeaytahtoh foomahray*]	no smoking
vietato gettare oggetti dal finestrino [*veeaytahtoh jettahray ohdjettee dahl feenesstreenoh*]	do not throw anything out of the window
vietato gettare rifiuti [*veeaytahtoh jettahray reefyootee*]	please do not throw your litter down
vietato l'ingresso [*veeaytahtoh leengresssoh*]	entrance forbidden

vietato parlare al manovratore [*veeaytahtoh pahrlahray ahl mahnohvrahtohray*]	please do not speak to the driver
vietato toccare [*veeaytahtoh tockkahray*]	do not touch

Vi JOURNEY

BY PLANE

airport	aeroporto [*ahayrohpohrtoh*]
aircraft, aeroplane	aereo [*ahayrayoh*]
airline company	compagnia aerea [*kompahnyeeah ahayrayah*]
air pocket	vuoto d'aria [*vooohtoh dahreeah*]
arrival	arrivo [*ahrreevoh*]
booking office	ufficio prenotazioni [*ooffeechoh praynohtahtseeohnay*]
(to) cancel	annullare [*ahnnoollahray*]
(to) change	cambiare [*kahmbeeahray*]
(to) check-in	presentarsi [*prayzentahrsee*]
(to) confirm	confermare [*konfehrmahray*]
conditioned air	aria condizionata [*ahreeah kondeetseeohnahtah*]
connection	coincidenza [*koheencheedentzah*]
customs	dogana [*dohgahnah*]
daily line	linea giornaliera [*leenayah jorrnahleeayrah*]
(to) declare	dichiarare [*deekeeahrahray*]
departure	partenza [*pahrtentsah*]
documents	documenti [*dohkoomentee*]
flight	volo [*vohloh*]
goods	merce [*mehrchay*]
helicopter	elicottero [*ayleekohttayroh*]
hijacking	dirottamento aereo [*deerottahmentoh ahayrayoh*]
(to) land	atterrare [*ahttehrrahray*]
landing	atterraggio [*ahttehrrahdjoh*]
luggage	bagagli [*bahgahlyee*]
luggage trolley	carrello portabagagli [*kahrrellloh porrtahbahgahlyee*]
parachute	paracadute [*pahrahkahdootay*]
passenger	passeggero [*pahssaydjayroh*]
passport	passaporto [*pahssahpohrtoh*]
pilot	pilota [*peelohtah*]
reservation	prenotazione [*praynohtahtseeohnay*]
runway	pista di decollo [*peestah dee daykollloh*]
seat	sedile [*saydeelay*]
suitcase	valigia [*vahleejah*]
(to) take off	decollare [*daykolllahray*]
ticket (single/return)	biglietto (di andata/di andata e di ritorno) [*beelyettoh dee ahndahtah ay reetornoh*]
twin-engined plane	bimotore [*beemohtohray*]

I'm here on holiday	Sono qui in vacanza [*sohnoh kwee een vahkahntsah*]
I'm here on business	Sono qui per affari [*sohnoh kwee pehr ahffahree*]
What time does the plane take off?	A che ora parte l'aereo? [*ah kay ohrah pahrtay lahyarayoh?*]
Is there a flight to Rome?	C'è un volo per Roma? [*chay oon vohloh pehr rohmah?*]
What time does it arrive in Rome?	A che ora arriva a Roma? [*ah kay ohrah ahrreevah ah rohmah?*]
Is it a direct flight?	È un volo diretto? [*ai oon vohloh deerettoh?*]
How long does it take to fly from X to Rome?	Quanto dura il volo da X a Roma? [*kwahntoh doorah eel vohloh dah X ah rohmah?*]
I'd like a ticket to Rome	Vorrei un biglietto per Roma [*vohrraiee oon beelyettoh pehr rohmah*]
How much is the return ticket?	Quanto costa il biglietto di andata e ritorno? [*kwahntoh kohstah eel beelyettoh dee ahndahtah ay reetornoh?*]
What's the flight number?	Qual è il numero del volo? [*kwahlay ai eel noomayroh dell vohloh?*]
I'd like to change my reservation on flight number...	Vorrei cambiare la mia prenotazione sul volo numero... [*vohrraiee kahmbeeahray lah meeah praynohtahtseeohnay sool vohloh noomayroh...*]
I'd like to confirm my reservation on flight number...	Vorrei confermare la mia prenotazione sul volo numero... [*vohrraiee konfehrmahray lah...*]
Where are the luggage trolleys?	Dove sono i carrelli portabagagli? [*dohvay sohnoh ee kahrrellee portahbahgahlyee?*]
I'd like to deposit my luggage	Vorrei lasciare in deposito il mio bagaglio [*vohrraiee lahshahray een daypohzeetoh eel meeoh bahgahlyoh*]
How many kilos of luggage are we allowed to take?	Quanti chili di bagagli si possono portare? [*kwahntee keelee dee bahgahlyee see possohnoh porrtahray?*]
Is there a bus to the airport?	C'è un autobus per l'aeroporto? [*chai oon owtohboos pehr lahayrohpohrtoh?*]
Where can I get a taxi?	Dove posso prendere un taxi? [*dohvay possho prendayray oon taxi?*]
Where can I hire a car?	Dove posso noleggiare una macchina? [*dohvay possoh nohlaydjahray oonah mahkkeenah?*]
Due to a sudden pilots' strike the departure is delayed	Causa un improvviso sciopero dei piloti la partenza è rimandata [*kowzah oon eemprovveezoh shohpayroh dayee peelohtee lah pahrtentsah ai reemahndahtah*]
There is a suitcase missing	Manca una valigia [*mahngkah oonah vahleejah*]

BY CAR

The motorway system in Italy is excellent, but a toll must be paid.
At the entrance to the motorway you are given a ticket showing where you joined the motorway. At the exit you pay according to the distance travelled.
Minor roads are not so well maintained and in winter snow-chains may be required.
In case of breakdown dial 116 for the ACI (Automobile Club d'Italia) which is affiliated to the AA and the RAC. Their nearest office will be informed and assistance will be sent as soon as possible.
Motorists must carry a triangular warning sign.

(to) accelerate	accelerare [*ahchchaylayrahray*]
accelerator	acceleratore [*ahchchaylayrahtohray*]
accessories	accessori [*ahchchesssohree*]
air filter	filtro dell'aria [*feeltroh dayl ahreeah*]
antifreeze	antigelo [*annteedjayloh*]
axle grease	lubrificante [*loobreefeekhantay*]
battery	batteri [*bahttayreeah*]
(to) be short of petrol	(essere in) riserva [*ehsssayray een reesehrvah*]
body	carrozzeria [*kahrrotzayreeah*]
bonnet	cofano [*kohfahnoh*]
(to) brake	frenare [*fraynahray*]
brake	freno [*fraynoh*]
break-down	guasto [*gwahstoh*]
brake light	freccia di stop [*freychcheeah dee stop*]
breakdown van	carro attrezzi [*kharroh ahttretzee*]
bumper	paraurti [*pahrahoortee*]
carburettor	carburatore [*kahrboorahtohray*]
car-hire	noleggio auto [*nohlaydjoh owtoh*]
car-park attendant	parcheggiatore [*pahrkaydjahtohray*]
car radio-set	autoradio [*owtohrahdeeoh*]
carrier	portapacchi [*pohrtahpahkkee*]
(to) change gear	cambiare marcia [*kahmbeeahray mahrchah*]
clutch	frizione [*freetseeohnay*]
coil-ignition	spinterogeno [*speentayrohjaynoh*]
(to) collide	investire [*eenvessteeray*]
collision	investimento [*eenvessteementoh*]
consumption	consumo [*konsoomoh*]
cubic capacity	cilindrata [*cheeleendrahtah*]
cylinder	cilindro [*cheeleendroh*]
dazzling light	faro abbagliante [*fahroh ahbbahlyahntay*]
diesel oil pump	gasolio [*gahsohlyeeoh*]

differential	differenziale [*deeffayrentzeeahlay*]
dimming light	faro anabbagliante [*fahroh ahnahbbahlyahntay*]
(to) drive	guidare [*gweedahray*]
driver	guidatore [*gweedahtohray*]
driving licence	patente di guida [*pahtayntay dee gweedah*]
driving mirror	specchietto retrovisivo [*speckkeeayttoh raytrohveezeevoh*]
engine	motore [*mohtohray*]
exhaust	tubo di scappamento [*tooboh dee skahppahmentoh*]
fill: fill it up!	pieno: faccia il pieno! [*peeaynoh: fahchchah eel peeaynoh*]
filling station	distributore di benzina [*deestreebootohray dee bendzeenay*]
fitting	guarnizione [*gwahrneetseeohnay*]
fog lights	faro antinebbia [*fahroh ahnteenebbeeah*]
foot brake	freno a pedale [*fraynoh ah paydahlay*]
garage	autorimessa [*owtohreemessah*]
(to) gear	ingranare [*eengrahnahray*]
gear	marcia [*mahrchah*]
gear lever	leva del cambio [*layvah dayl kahmbeeoh*]
(to) grease	ingrassare [*eengrahssahray*]
hand-brake	freno a mano [*fraynoh ah mahnoh*]
head light	fanale anteriore [*fahnahlay ahntayreeohray*]
highway	autostrada [*owtohstrahdah*]
horn	clacson [*klahksonn*]
horse power (HP)	cavalli (HP) [*kahvahllee*]
inner tube	camera d'aria [*kahmayrah dahreeah*]
in neutral	in folle [*een folllay*]
jack	crick [*kreek*]
left hand drive	guida a sinistra [*gweedah ah seeneestrah*]
light	fanalino, faro [*fahnahleenoh fahroh*]
light indicator	lampeggiatore [*lahmpaydjahtohray*]
luggage grid	portabagagli [*porrtahbahgahlyee*]
(to) manœuvre	fare manovra [*fahray mahnohvrah*]
mechanic	meccanico [*meckkahneekoh*]
methane gas pump	metano [*maytahnoh*]
mixture	miscela [*meeshaylah*]
motor	motore [*mohtohray*]
mudguard	parafango [*pahrahfahnggoh*]
number plate	targa [*tahrgah*]
oil	olio [*ohleeoh*]
(to) park	parcheggiare [*pahrkaydjahray*]
parking	parcheggio [*pahrkaydjoh*]
pedal	pedale [*paydahlay*]
petrol	benzina [*bendzeenah*]
petrol-tank	serbatoio della benzina [*sehrbahtohyoh dayllah bendzeenah*]

piston pistone [*peestohnay*]
policeman vigile [*veejeelay*]
pump pompa [*pompah*]
(to) puncture forare [*fohrahray*]
quarter light diflettore [*dayflayttohray*]
racing car automobile da corsa [*owtohmohbeelay dah korrsah*]
radiator radiatore [*rahdeeahtohray*]
rear light fanale posteriore [*fahnahlay posstayreeohray*]
rear mirror specchietto retrovisore [*spaykkeeayttoh raytrohveesohray*]
reflector catarifrangente [*kahtahreefrahndjentay*]
registration card carta di circolazione [*kahrtah dee cheerkohlatseeohnay*]
repair riparazione [*reepahrahtseeohnay*]
reverse gear retromarcia [*raytrohmahrcheeah*]
road accident incidente stradale [*eencheedayntay strahdahlay*]
run-down battery batteria scarica [*bahttayreeah skahreekah*]
safety device against theft antifurto [*ahnteefoortoh*]
seat sedile [*saydeelay*]
seat-belt cintura di sicurezza [*cheentoorah dee seekooretsah*]
service station officina di riparazioni [*offfeecheenah dee reepahrahtseeohnee*]
side light fanale laterale [*fahnahlay lahtayrahlay*]
silencer marmitta [*mahrmeettah*]
spare wheel ruota di scorta [*rooohtah dee skorrtah*]
sparking-plug candela [*kahndaylah*]
speed velocità [*vaylohcheetah*]
(to) start the engine avviare il motore [*ahvveeahray eel mohtohray*]
starter avviamento [*ahvveeahmentoh*]
steering column sterzo [*stayrtzoh*]
steering wheel volante [*vohlahntay*]
tank serbatoio [*sehrbahtohyoh*]
(to) tow rimorchiare [*reemorrkeeahray*]
towing forbidden proibito farsi rimorchiare [*prohheebeetoh fahrsee reemorrkeeahray*]
traffic lights semaforo [*saymahfohroh*]
trailer rimorchio [*reemorrkeeoh*]
triangle triangolo [*treeahnggohloh*]
tyre gomma [*gommah*]
valve valvola [*vahlvohlah*]
washing lavaggio [*lahvahdjoh*]
wheel ruota [*rooohtah*]
windscreen wiper tergicristallo [*tehrdjeekreestahlloh*]
zebra crossing strisce pedonali [*streeshay paydohnahlee*]

ROAD SIGNS

Accendere i fari in galleria	Use headlights in tunnel
Dare la precedenza	Give way
Deviazione	Diversion
Circonvallazione	Ring road
Piazzola di sosta	Lay-by
Passaggio a livello	Level crossing
Pericolo	Danger
Rallentare	Slow down
Senso unico	One way
Strada con diritto di precedenza	Priority road
Strada senza uscita	No through road
Zona pedonale	Pedestrian zone

ASKING FOR DIRECTIONS

Have you a map of this town?	Ha una pianta di questa città? [*ah oonah peeahntah dee kwesstah cheettah?*]
Can you tell me the way to...?	Può indicarmi la strada per...? [*poooh eendeekahrmee lah strahdah pehr...?*]
How can I find this place?	Come posso trovare questo posto? [*kohmay posssoh trohvahray kwesstoh posstoh?*]
Which road do I take for...?	Quale strada devo prendere per...? [*kwahlay strahdah dayvoh prendayray pehr...?*]
Is this the turning for...?	Devo girare qui per...? [*dayvoh jeerahray kwee pehr...?*]
Where can I park?	Dove posso posteggiare? [*dohvay posssoh posstaydjahray?*]
How long can I park here?	Quanto tempo posso restare qui? [*kwahntoh tempoh posssoh resstahray kwee?*]
Where's the entrance to the highway?	Dov'è l'ingresso all'autostrada? [*dohvay leengressoh ahllowtohstrahdah?*]

AT A FILLING STATION

Full tank, please	Il pieno, per favore [*eel peeaynoh pehr fahvohray*]
Give me ... litres of petrol	Mi dia ... litri di benzina [*mee deeah ... leetree dee bendzeenah*]
Water and oil, please	Acqua e olio, per favore [*ahkkwah ay ohleeoh, pehr fahvohray*]
Please check the brake fluid	Per favore controlli l'olio dei freni [*pehr fahvohray kontrolllee lohleeoh dayee fraynee*]

Would you check the tyre pressure?	Può controllare la pressione delle gomme? [*poooh kontrolllahray lah pressseeohnay delllay gommay?*]
Can you mend this puncture?	Può riparare questa foratura? [*poooh reepahrahray kwesstah fohrahtoorah*]
Wash and grease the car, please	Lavaggio e ingrassaggio, per favore [*lahvahdjoh ay eengrahssahdjoh pehr fahvohray*]
Would you please change one of the sparking plugs?	Potrebbe cambiarmi una candela? [*pohtraybbay kahmbeeahrmee oonah kahndaylah*]
The battery has run down	La batteria è scarica [*lah bahttayreeah ay skahreekah*]

BREAKDOWNS

My car has broken down. Where's the nearest garage?	Ho un guasto. Dov'è il garage più vicino? [*oh oon gwahstoh. dohvay eel garage peeoo veecheenoh?*]
Can you send a breakdown van?	Può mandare un carro attrezzi? [*poooh mandahray oon kahrroh ahttretzee?*]
Can you send a mechanic?	Può mandare un meccanico? [*poooh mahndahray oon meckkahneekoh?*]
The engine is overheating	Il motore è surriscaldato [*eel mohtohray ay soorreeskahldahtoh*]
Can you repair the damage at your garage?	Può eseguire la riparazione nella sua autorimessa? [*poooh ayzaygweeray lah reepahrahtserohnay nelllah sooah owtohreemesssah?*]
How much is it?	Quanto costa? [*kwahntoh kohstah?*]
How long will it take?	Quanto tempo occorre? [*kwahntoh tempoh ockkorrray?*]
I've run out of petrol	Sono rimasto senza benzina [*sohnoh reemahstoh sentsah bendzeenah*]
Can you sell me some?	Può vendermene un po'? [*poooh vendayrmaynay oon poh?*]
There is something wrong with...	Qualcosa non va con... [*kwahlkohsah nonn vah kon...*]

ROAD ACCIDENTS

I have had an accident	Ho avuto un incidente [*oh ahvootoh oon eencheedentay*]
Please come and fetch my car and tow it to your repair workshop	Per favore venite a prendere la mia macchina e rimorchiatela alla vostra officina [*pehr fahvohray vayneetay ah prendayray lah meeah mahkkeenah ay reemorrkeeahtaylah ahlllah vosstrah offfeecheenah*]
Please call the police	Per favore chiami la polizia [*pehr fahvohray keeahmee lah pohleetseeah*]

The car number was...	La targa era... [*lah tahrgah ayrah...*]
Where's the nearest telephone?	Dov'è il telefono più vicino? [*dohvay eel taylayfohnoh peeoo veecheenoh?*]
Call an ambulance, quickly	Chiamate un'ambulanza, presto [*keeahmahtay oon ahmboolahntzah, presstoh*]
You ran into me. Give me your name and address	Lei mi ha investito. Mi dia nome e indirizzo [*layee mee ah eenvessteetoh. mee deeah nohmay ay eendeereetzoh*]
I've crashed my car	Ho distrutto la macchina [*oh deestroottoh lah mahkkeenah*]
He did not give way	Non ha dato la precedenza [*nonn ah dahtoh lah praychaydentsah*]
What's your insurance company?	Qual è la sua assicurazione? [*kwahlay lah sooah ahsseekoorahtseeohnay*]
Here is my name and the address of my insurance agent	Ecco il mio nome e l'indirizzo della mia assicurazione [*ekkoh eel meeoh nohmay ay leendeeretzoh delllah meeah ahsseekoorahtseeohnay*]

> Third party insurance is compulsory. It is best to carry an international Green Card which you should be able to obtain from your insurance.

CAR HIRE

I want to hire a car	Voglio noleggiare una macchina [*vohlyoh nohlaydjahray oonah mahkkeenah*]
What's the charge per day?	Qual è la tariffa giornaliera? [*kwahlay lah tahreeffah jorrnahleeayrah?*]
What's the charge per kilometre?	Qual è la tariffa al chilometro? [*kwahlay lah tahreeffah ahl keelohmaytroh?*]
What's the deposit?	Qual è il deposito? [*kwahlay eel daypohzeetoh?*]
How do I operate the controls?	Come funzionano i comandi? [*kohmay foontseeohnahnoh ee kohmahndee?*]
I want full insurance	Voglio l'assicurazione completa [*vohlyoh lahsseekoorahtseeohnay komplaytah*]

ITALIAN NUMBERPLATES

AG	Agrigento
AL	Alessandria
AN	Ancona
AO	Aosta
AP	Ascoli Piceno
AQ	L'Aquila
AR	Arezzo
AT	Asti
AV	Avellino
BA	Bari
BG	Bergamo
BL	Belluno
BN	Benevento
BO	Bologna
BR	Brindisi
BS	Brescia
BZ	Bolzano
CA	Cagliari
CB	Campobasso
CE	Caserta
CH	Chieti
CL	Caltanissetta
CN	Cuneo
CO	Como
CR	Cremona
CS	Cosenza
CT	Catania
CZ	Catanzaro
EN	Enna
FE	Ferrara
FG	Foggia
FI	Firenze
FO	Forlì
FR	Frosinone
GE	Genova
GO	Gorizia
GR	Grosseto
IM	Imperia
IS	Isernia
LE	Lecce
LI	Livorno
LT	Latina
LU	Lucca
MC	Macerata
ME	Messina
MI	Milano
MN	Mantova
MO	Modena
MS	Massa Carrara
MT	Matera
NA	Napoli
NO	Novara
NU	Nuoro
OR	Oristano
PA	Palermo
PC	Piacenza
PD	Padova
PE	Pescara
PG	Perugia
PI	Pisa
PN	Pordenone
PR	Parma
PS	Pesaro
PT	Pistoia
PV	Pavia
PZ	Potenza
RA	Ravenna
RC	Reggio Calabria
RE	Reggio Emilia
RG	Ragusa
RI	Rieti
RO	Rovigo
ROMA	Roma
SA	Salerno
SI	Siena
SO	Sondrio
SP	La Spezia
SR	Siracusa
SS	Sassari
SV	Savona
TA	Taranto
TE	Teramo
TN	Trento
TO	Torino
TP	Trapani
TR	Terni
TS	Trieste
TV	Treviso
UD	Udine
VA	Varese
VC	Vercelli
VE	Venezia
VI	Vicenza
VR	Verona
VT	Viterbo

BY TRAIN

TYPES OF TRAINS

Locale (L)/Accelerato (A)
[*lohkahlay/ahchchaylayrahtoh*]
slow trains which stop at all small stations.

Diretto (D)
[*deerayttoh*]
makes frequent local stops.

Espresso (EXP)/Direttissimo
[*esspresssoh/deeraytteesseemoh*]
Long-distance trains, stopping at main stations.

Intercity (IC)
is a fast train with very few stops.

Rapido (R)
[*rahpeedoh*]
Long-distance express train stopping at major cities only.

TEE
[*teeayay*]
Trans Europ Express; a luxury, international service with first class only. Additional fare and reservation required.

(to) arrive	arrivare [*ahrreevahray*]
arrival	arrivo [*ahrreevoh*]
(to) board	salire [*sahleeray*]
booking office	sportello [*sporrtellloh*]
cancelled train	treno soppresso [*traynoh sopprayssoh*]
carriage	vettura [*vettoorah*]
(to) change class	cambiare classe [*kahmbeeahray klasssay*]
(to) change train	cambiare treno [*kahmbeeahray traynoh*]
compartment	scompartimento [*skompahrteementoh*]
conductor	capotreno [*kahpohtraynoh*]
connection	coincidenza [*koheencheedentzah*]
corridor	corridoio [*korrreedoyoh*]
departure	partenza [*pahrtentsah*]
emergency brake	segnale d'allarme [*saynyahlay dahllahrmay*]
engine	locomotiva [*lohkohmohteevah*]
engine driver	macchinista [*mahkkeeneestah*]
entrance	entrata [*entrahtah*]
exchange desk	ufficio cambio [*ooffeechoh kahmbeeoh*]
exit	uscita [*oosheetah*]
fare	prezzo [*pretsoh*]
first class waiting-room	sala d'attesa di prima classe [*sahla datttaysah dee preemah klasssay*]
gates closed/open	barriere abbassate/alzate [*bahrreeayray ahbbahssahtay/ahltzahtay*]

(to) get off	scendere [*shendayray*]
(to) get on	salire [*sahleeray*]
goods train	treno merci [*traynoh mehrchee*]
holiday ticket	biglietto festivo [*beelyettoh faysteevoh*]
information office	ufficio informazioni [*ooffeechoh eenforrmahtseeohnee*]
lavatory	ritirata [*reeteerahtah*]
(to) leave	partire [*pahrteeray*]
left luggage office	deposito bagagli [*daypohzeetoh bahgahlyee*]
level crossing	passaggio a livello [*pahssahdjoh ah leevellloh*]
locomotive	locomotiva [*lohkohmohteevah*]
lost property office	ufficio oggetti smarriti [*ooffeechoh ohdjettee smahrreetee*]
luggage	bagaglio [*bahgahlyoh*]
luggage ticket	scontrino [*skontreenoh*]
luggage van	bagagliaio [*bahgahlyahyoh*]
lunch pack	cestino da viaggio [*chaysteenoh dah veeahdjoh*]
(to) miss the train	perdere il treno [*pehrdayray eel traynoh*]
passenger	passeggero [*pahssaydjayroh*]
pillow	cuscino [*koosheenoh*]
platform	binario [*beenahreeoh*]
porter	facchino [*fahkkeenoh*]
relief train	treno straordinario [*traynoh strahohrdeenahreeoh*]
reserved seat	posto riservato [*posstoh reesehrvahtoh*]
restaurant car	vettura ristorante [*vettoorah reestorahntay*]
return ticket	biglietto di andata e ritorno [*beelyettoh dee ahndahtah ay reetorrnoh*]
single ticket	biglietto d'andata [*beelyettoh dahndahtah*]
sleeper booking	prenotazione cuccette [*praynohtahtseeohnay koochchettay*]
sleeping car	carrozza letto [*kahrrotzah lettoh*]
smoking compartment	scompartimento per fumatori [*skohmpahrteementoh pehr foomahtohree*]
starting signal	segnale di partenza [*saynyahlay dee pahrtentsah*]
station	stazione [*stahtseeohnay*]
station master	capostazione [*kahpohstahtseeohnay*]
(to) stop	fermarsi [*fehrmahrsee*]
subway	sottopassaggio [*sottohpahssahdjoh*]
ticket	biglietto [*beelyettoh*]
ticket collector	controllore [*kontrollloray*]
ticket office	biglietteria [*beelyettayreeah*]
timetable	orario [*ohrahreeoh*]
train	treno [*traynoh*]
travel agency	agenzia viaggi [*ahjentzeeah veeahdjee*]

trolley	carrello portabagagli [*kahrrellloh pohrtahbahgahlyee*]
tunnel	galleria [*gahllayreeah*]
trunk	baule [*bahoolay*]
valid	valevole [*vahlayvohlay*]
waiting room	sala d'aspetto [*sahlah dahspettoh*]
window	finestrino [*feenaystreenoh*]

TICKETS

Where's the booking office?	Dov'è la biglietteria? [*dohvay lah beelyettayreeah?*]
One second class return ticket to Rome, please	Un biglietto di andata e ritorno di seconda classe per Roma, per favore [*oon beelyettoh dee ahndahtah ay reetohrnoh dee saykohndah clahssay pehr rohmah, pehr fahvohray*]
I want to take the intercity, what's the difference in the price?	Desidero prendere l'Intercity, qual è il supplemento? [*dayseedayroh prendayray l'intercity kwahlay eel soopplaymentoh*]
I want to book a berth	Desidero prenotare una cuccetta [*dayseedayroh praynohtahray oonah koochchayttah*]
I want a weekly ticket, please	Desidero un abbonamento settimanale, per favore [*dayseedayroh oon ahbbbohnahmentoh saytteemahnahlay, pehr fahvohray*]

INFORMATION

When is the next train to Rome?	Quando parte il prossimo treno per Roma? [*kwahndoh pahrtay eel prossseemoh traynoh pehr rohmah?*]
Is it a through train?	È un treno diretto? [*ay oon traynoh deerayttoh?*]
Is there a connection to...	C'è una coincidenza per... [*chay oonah koheencheedentzah pehr...*]
Do I have to change train?	Devo cambiare treno? [*dayvoh kahmbeeahray traynoh?*]
What platform does the train for Rome leave from?	Da che binario parte il treno per Roma? [*dah kay beenahreeoh pahrtay eel traynoh pehr rohmah?*]
When does it arrive?	Quando arriva? [*kwahndoh ahrreevah?*]
Does this train go directly to...?	Questo treno va direttamente a... [*kwaystoh traynoh vah deerayttahmentay ah...?*]
Where's the travel agency?	Dov'è l'agenzia di viaggi? [*dohvay lahjentzeeah dee veeahdjee?*]

ON THE TRAIN

Is there a seat free?	C'è un posto libero? [*chay oon posstoh leebayroh?*]
Yes/no/it is taken	Sì/no/è occupato [*see/noh/ay okkoopahtoh*]
Excuse me. May I get by?	Scusi. Posso passare? [*skoozee. Posssoh pahssahray?*]
Would you mind closing the window?	Le dispiace chiudere il finestrino? [*lay deespeeahchay keeoodayray eel feenaystreenoh?*]
May I smoke?	Posso fumare? [*posssoh foomahray?*]
Would you mind keeping my place for a moment?	Può tenermi il posto un momento? [*poooh taynayrmee eel posstoh oon mohmayntoh?*]
Excuse me, may I put the light off?	Scusi posso spegnere la luce? [*skoozee posssoh spaynyayray lah loochay?*]
Here's the ticket-collector	Ecco il controllore [*ekkoh eel kontrolllohray*]
Is there a supplement on this ticket?	C'è un supplemento su questo biglietto? [*chay oon soopplaymentoh soo kwesstoh beelyettoh?*]
The train is on schedule/is ahead/is delayed?	Il treno è in orario/in anticipo/in ritardo? [*eel traynoh ay een ohrahreeoh/een ahnteecheepoh/een reetahrdoh?*]
Where's the sleeping car?	Dov'è il vagone letto? [*dohvay eel vagohnay lettoh?*]
Where's my berth?	Dov'è la mia cuccetta? [*dohvay lah meeah koochchettah?*]

LUGGAGE

Porter!	Facchino! [*fahkkeenoh!*]
Please take my luggage to a taxi	Per favore porti i miei bagagli al taxi [*pehr fahvohray pohrtee ee meeayee bahgahlyee ahl taxee*]
How much is that?	Quant'è? [*kwahntay?*]
Are there any luggage trolleys?	Ci sono dei carrelli per i bagagli? [*chee sohnoh dayee karrellee pehr ee bahgahlyee?*]
My luggage has not arrived	I miei bagagli non sono arrivati [*ee meeayee bahgahlyee nonn sohnoh arreevahtee*]
Where is the left-luggage office?	Dov'è il deposito bagagli? [*dohvay eel daypohzeetoh bahgahlyee?*]
Where do I check in my suitcases?	Dove posso consegnare le mie valigie? [*dohvay posssoh konsaynyahray lay meeay vahleejay?*]

BY BOAT

anchor	ancora [*ahnkkohrah*]
berth	cuccetta [*koochchettah*]
boat	barca [*bahrkah*]; battello [*bahttellloh*]
cabin	cabina [*kahbeenah*]
(to) call at a port	toccare un porto [*tockkahray oon porrtoh*]
(to) cast anchor	gettare l'ancora [*jettahray lahngkohrah*]
coast	costa [*kohstah*]
course	rotta [*rottah*]
crossing	traversata [*trahvehrsahtah*]
cruise	crociera [*krohchayrah*]
deck	ponte [*pohntay*]
departure	partenza [*pahrtentsah*]
(to) disembark	sbarcare [*sbahrkahray*]
(to) embark	imbarcarsi [*eembahrkahrsee*]
embarkation	imbarco [*eembahrkoh*]
ferry-boat	traghetto [*trahghettoh*]
(to) go ashore	sbarcare [*sbahrkahray*]
harbour port	porto [*porrtoh*]
hold	stiva [*steevah*]
knot	nodo [*nohdoh*]
life-belt	salvagente [*sahlvahjentay*]
life boat	canotto di salvataggio [*kahnottoh dee sahlvahtahdjoh*]
light-house	faro [*fahroh*]
on board	a bordo [*ah borrdoh*]
pier	molo [*mohloh*]
pitching	beccheggio [*beckkaydjoh*]
port-hole	oblò [*ohbloh*]
prow	prua [*prooah*]
quay	banchina di porto [*bahngkeenah dee porrtoh*]
rolling	rullio [*roolleeoh*]
rudder	timone [*teemohnay*]
sail	vela [*vaylah*]
(to) sail	navigare [*nahveegahray*]
(to) set sail	salpare [*sahlpahray*]
sailing boat	barca a vela [*bahrkah ah vaylah*]
sailing company	compagnia di navigazione [*kompahnyeeah dee nahveegahtseeohnay*]
sailor	marinaio [*mahreenahyoh*]
sea	mare [*mahray*]
sea-sickness	mal di mare [*mahl dee mahray*]
sea voyage	viaggio per mare [*veeahdjoh pehr mahray*]
ship	nave [*nahvay*]
siren	sirena [*seeraynah*]

stern	poppa [*poppah*]
tide	marea [*mahrayah*]
(to) tow	rimorchiare [*reemorrkeeahray*]
tug	rimorchiatore [*reemorrkeeahtohray*]
wave	onda [*ondah*]

I want to book a second class cabin with two berths on the ship sailing on the 7th of June from the port of...	Desidero prenotare una cabina di seconda classe a due letti sulla nave in partenza il 7 giugno dal porto di... [*dayseedayroh praynohtahray oonah kahbeenah dee saykohndah klahssay ah dooay lettee soollah nahvay een pahrtentsah eel settay joonyoh dahl porrtoh dee...*]
What time does the ship weigh anchor?	A che ora si salpa? [*ah kay ohrah see sahlpah?*]
How long does the crossing last?	Quanto dura la traversata? [*kwahntoh doorah lah trahverrsahtah?*]
We'll arrive in two hours	Fra due ore arriveremo [*frah dooay ohray ahrreevayraymoh*]
What does it cost to ferry a car?	Quanto costa il traghetto di un'automobile? [*kwahntoh kohstah eel trahghettoh dee oon owtohmohbeelay?*]
What time does the ferry-boat leave?	Quando parte il traghetto? [*kwahndoh pahrtay eel trahghettoh?*]
The ferry goes twice daily, and connects with the train at...	Il traghetto parte due volte al giorno in coincidenza col treno ... alle... [*eel trahghettoh pahrtay dooay vohltay ahl jorrnoh een koheencheedentzah kohl traynoh ... ahllay...*]
Where has my luggage been put?	Dove sono stati messi i miei bagagli? [*dohvay sohnoh stahtee messsee ee meeayee bahgahlyee?*]
Do you suffer from sea-sickness?	Soffre il mal di mare? [*soffray eel mahl dee mahray?*]
I want to make a tour through the canals of the town	Voglio fare un giro in battello sui canali della città [*vollyoh fahray oon jeeroh een bahttellloh sooee kahnahlee dayllah cheettah*]
What is the fare?	Quanto costa il biglietto? [*kwahntoh kohstah eel beelyettoh?*]

TRAVELLING ON LOCAL TRANSPORT

BY COACH

Italians refer to a coach either as «un pullman» or «una corriera».

Where do I catch the coach for...?	Dove posso prendere l'autobus per...? [*dohvay posssoh prendayray eel poolmahn pehr...?*]
Does this coach stop at...?	Questo pullman si ferma a...? [*kwestoh poolmahn see fermah ah...?*]
What time does it leave?/arrive?	A che ora parte?/arriva? [*ah kay ohrah pahrtay?/ahrreevah?*]
Is there an overnight service to...?	C'è un servizio notturno per...? [*chay oon sehrveetseeoh nottoornoh pehr...?*]
How long does the journey take?	Quanto dura il viaggio? [*kwahntoh doorah eel veeahdjoh?*]

BY BUS

In many large towns, automatic ticket machines have replaced conductors on the buses, and a one-price fare is in operation. In some places the ticket machines themselves have been superseded and you have to buy a ticket at a «tabaccheria» before you get on the bus.

I'd like a booklet of tickets	Vorrei un blocchetto di biglietti [*vorrayee oon blockkayttoh dee beelyeettee*]
Is there a bus to...?	C'è un autobus per...? [*chay oon owtohbooss pehr...?*]
Which bus goes to...?	Quale autobus va a...? [*kwahlay owtohbooss vah ah...?*]
How many bus stops are there to...	Quante fermate ci sono fino a... [*kwahntay fehrmahtay chee sohnoh feenoh ah...*]
Where do I get off?	Dove devo scendere? [*dohvay dayvoh shendayray?*]
Let me off here, please	Mi faccia scendere qui, per favore [*mee fahchchah shendayray qwee pehr fahvohray*]

BY UNDERGROUND

Milan and Rome both have an underground railway system, «la metropolitana» or «il metrò». In both cities, the fare is always the same, irrespective of the distance you travel.
Signs to look for:

Ai Binari	to the platforms
Biglietteria	ticket office
Gabinetti	toilets

Where's the nearest underground station?	Dov'è la stazione metropolitana più vicina? [*dohvay lah stahtseeohnay maytrohpohleetahnah peeoo veecheenah?*]
Which line should I take for...?	Che linea devo prendere per...? [*kay leenayah dayvoh prendayray pehr...?*]
Where do I change for...?	Dove cambio per..? [*dohvay cahmbeeoh pehr...?*]

Vii OFFICES AND SERVICES

AT THE CUSTOMS

bag	borsa [*borrsah*]
brief-case	cartella [*kahrtellah*]
collective passport	passaporto collettivo [*pahssahporrtoh kolllaytteevoh*]
contraband	contrabbando [*kontrabbahndoh*]
control	controllo [*kontrollloh*]
customs duty	tassa di dogana [*tahssah dee dohgahnah*]
customs house	ufficio di dogana [*ooffeechoh dee dohgahnah*]
customs inspection	visita di dogana [*veezeetah dee dohgahnah*]
customs officer	doganiere [*dohgahneeayray*]
(to) declare	dichiarare [*deekeeahrahray*]
export duty	dogana d'esportazione [*dohgahnah dessporrtahtseeohnay*]
free of customs duty	esente da dogana [*ayzentay dah dohgahnah*]
handbag	borsetta [*borrsayttah*]
(to) inspect	controllare [*kontrolllahray*]
inspector	controllore [*kontrolllohray*]
luggage	bagaglio [*bahgahlyoh*]
passport	passaporto [*pahssahporrtoh*]
personal effects	effetti personali [*effettee pehrsohnahlee*]
receipt	ricevuta [*reechayvootah*]
subject to duty	soggetto a dogana [*sohdjettoh ah dohgahnah*]
suitcase	valigia [*vahleejah*]
trunk	baule [*bahoolay*]

Do you have anything to declare?	Ha qualcosa da dichiarare? [*ah kwahlkohsah dah deekeeahrahray?*]
I have nothing to declare	Non ho niente da dichiarare [*nonn oh neeentay dah deekeeahrahray*]
Only personal effects	Solo effetti personali [*sohloh effettee pehrsohnahlee*]
I've a bottle of whisky	Ho una bottiglia di whisky [*oh oonah botteelyah dee whisky*]
Must I pay on this?	Devo pagare per questo? [*dayvoh pahgahray pehr kwesstoh?*]
There is no duty on those	Quelli sono esenti da dogana [*kwelllee sohnoh ayzentee dah dohgahnah*]

Have you paid customs duty on this camera?	Avete pagato la tassa di dogana per questa macchina fotografica? [*ahvaytay pahgahtoh lah tahssah dee dohgahnah pehr kwesstah mahkkeenah fohtohgrahfeekah?*]
How much money have you got?	Quanto denaro ha? [*kwahntoh daynahroh ah?*]
Have you any other money besides that marked on the form?	Ha altra valuta oltre quella segnata sul modulo? [*ah ahltrah vahlootah olltray kwelllah saynyahtah sool mohdooloh?*]
Please open this bag	Per favore, apra questa borsa [*pehr fahvohray ahprah kwesstah borrsah*]
All right, you may go	Va bene, può andare [*vah baynay poooh ahndahray*]

BANK

account	conto [*kontoh*]
bank charges	spese bancarie [*spaysay bahngkahreeay*]
bank draft	assegno circolare [*ahssaynyoh cheerkohlahray*]
bearer cheque	assegno al portatore [*ahssaynyoh ahl porrtahtohray*]
bill of exchange	cambiale [*kahmbeeahlay*]
bill payable at maturity	cambiale pagabile a scadenza [*kahmbeeahlay pahgahbeelay ah skahdentsah*]
bill payable at sight	cambiale pagabile a vista [*kahmbeeahlay pahgahbeelay ah veestah*]
bounced	scoperto [*skohpehrtoh*]
(to) cash	incassare [*eenkahssahray*]
cheque	assegno bancario [*ahssaynyoh bahngkahreeyoh*]
cheque book	libretto d'assegni [*leebrayttoh dahssaynyee*]
counter	sportello [*sporrtellloh*]
(to) credit	accreditare [*ahkkraydeetahray*]
credit card	carta di credito [*kahrtah dee kraydeetoh*]
crossed cheque	assegno sbarrato [*ahssaynyoh sbahrrahtoh*]
currency	moneta circolante [*mohnaytah cheerkohlahntay*]
current account	conto corrente [*kontoh korrrentay*]
(to) deposit	depositare [*daypohzeetahray*]
devaluation	svalutazione [*svahlootahtseeohnay*]
(to) endorse a cheque	girare un assegno [*jeerahray oon ahssaynyoh*]
exchange	cambio [*kahmbeeoh*]
exchange broker	cambiavalute [*kahmbeeahvahlootay*]
exchange rate	corso del cambio [*korrsoh dayl kahmbeeoh*]
free of taxation	esente da tasse [*ayzentay dah tahssay*]
(to) insure	assicurare [*ahsseekoorahray*]
insurance	assicurazione [*ahsseekoorahtseeohnay*]
interest rate	tasso d'interesse [*tahssoh deentayresssay*]
money order	vaglia [*vahlyah*]
mortgage	ipoteca [*eepohtaykah*]
night safe	cassa continua [*kahssah konteenooah*]
out of circulation	fuori corso [*fooohree korrsoh*]
payment	pagamento [*pahgahmentoh*]
percentage	percentuale [*pehrchentooahlay*]
ready money	contante [*kontahntay*]
receipt	ricevuta [*reechayvootah*]
(to) refund	rimborsare [*reemborrsahray*]
rise	rialzo [*reeahltsoh*]

safe deposit-box	cassetta di sicurezza [*kahssettah dee seekooretsah*]
share	azione [*ahtseeohnay*]
Stock Exchange	Borsa [*borrsah*]
(to) withdraw	prelevare [*praylayvahray*]
untransferable cheque	assegno non trasferibile [*ahssaynyoh nonn trahsfayreebeelay*]

Where's the nearest bank?	Dov'è la banca più vicina? [*dohvay lah bahngkah peeoo veecheenah?*]
Is there an exchange office?	C'è un ufficio di cambio? [*chai oon ooffeechoh dee kahmbeeoh?*]
What's today's exchange rate?	Qual è il corso del cambio oggi? [*kwahl ai eel korrsoh dayl kahmbeeoh ohdjee?*]
I'd like to change 100 Pounds to Lire	Vorrei cambiare 100 sterline in lire [*vorrayee kahmbeeahray chentoh stehrleenay een leeray*]
I wish to cash a traveller's cheque	Vorrei incassare un traveller's cheque [*vorrayee eenkahssahray oon traveller's cheque*]
Please, give me two dollars in small change, the rest in banknotes	Per favore, mi dia due dollari in moneta spicciola, il resto in banconote [*pehr fahvohray mee deeah dooay dohllahree een mohnaytah speechchohlah eel resstoh een bahngkohnohtay*]
Have you any personal document?	Ha un documento personale? [*ah oon dohkoomentoh pehrsohnahlay?*]
Here is my passport	Ecco il mio passaporto [*ekkoh eel meeoh pahssahporrtoh*]
Sign this receipt, if you please	Per favore, firmi questa ricevuta [*pehr fahvohray feermee qwesstah reechayvootah*]
Can you telex my bank in London?	Può mandare un telex alla mia banca a Londra? [*pwo mahndahray oon telex ahllah meeah bahngkah ah lohndrah?*]
I want to credit this to my account	Desidero accreditare questo sul mio conto [*dayzeedayroh ahkkraydeetahray qwesstoh sool meeoh kontoh*]
I want to open an account	Desidero aprire un conto [*dayzeedayroh ahpreeray oon kontoh*]
I want to withdraw...lire	Desidero prelevare...lire [*dayzeedayroh praylayvahray...leeray*]
Where should I sign?	Dove devo firmare? [*dohvay dayvoh feermahray?*]

BUSINESS

account	conto [*kontoh*]
accountant	contabile [*kontahbeelay*]
addressee	destinatario [*dessteenahtahreeoh*]
advertising	pubblicità [*poobbleecheetah*]
agency	agenzia [*ahjentzeeah*]
agent	agente [*ahjentay*]
(to) agree	accordarsi [*ahkkorrdahrsee*]
agreement	accordo [*ahkkorrdoh*]
assets	(bilancio) attivo [*beelahnchoh ahtteevoh*]
assortment	assortimento [*ahssorrteementoh*]
auction	asta [*ahstah*]
bargain	occasione [*ockkahzeeohnay*]
bill of lading	polizza di carico [*pohleetsah dee kahreekoh*]
board of directors	consiglio [*konseelyoh*]
board of Trade	Ministero del Commercio [*meeneestayroh dayl kommehrchoh*]
boss	principale [*preencheepahlay*]
branch	filiale [*feeleeahlay*]
budget	bilancio preventivo [*beelahnchoh prayventeevoh*]
business consultant	commercialista [*kommehrchahleestah*]
(to) buy	comprare [*komprahray*]
cash	cassa, contanti [*kahssah, kontahntee*]
cashier	cassiere [*kahsseeayray*]
catalogue	catalogo [*kahtahlohgoh*]
certificate of origin	certificato d'origine [*chehrteefeekahtoh dohreejeenay*]
chamber of commerce	camera di commercio [*kahmayrah dee kommehrchoh*]
charter-party	contratto di noleggio [*kontrahttoh dee nohlaydjoh*]
cheap	a buon mercato [*ah booohn mehrkahtoh*]
(to) clear	sdoganare [*sdohgahnahray*]
clearance sale	vendita di liquidazione [*vendeetah dee leekweedahtseeohnay*]
client	cliente [*kleeentay*]
commerce	commercio [*kommehrchoh*]
company	società [*sohcheeaytah*]
complaint	reclamo [*rayklahmoh*]
contract	contratto [*kontrahttoh*]
correspondence	corrispondenza [*korreespondentsah*]
correspondent	corrispondente [*korreespondentay*]
(to) cost	costare [*kohstahray*]
cost	costo [*kohstoh*]
cost-price	prezzo di costo [*pretsoh dee kohstoh*]
customer	cliente [*kleeentay*]

damage to third persons	assicurazione per danni contro terzi [*ahsseekoorahtseeohnay pehr dahnnee kontroh tehrtsee*]
(to) deal	negoziare [*naygohtseeahray*]
(to) debit	addebitare [*ahddaybeetahray*]
debit, debt	debito [*daybeetoh*]
debtor	debitore [*daybeetohray*]
delivery	consegna [*konsaynyah*]
delivery-note	lettera di carico [*lettayrah dee kahreekoh*]
demand	domanda [*dohmahndah*]
(to) deposit	depositare [*daypohzeetahray*]
discount	sconto [*skontoh*]
double entry	partita doppia [*pahrteetah doppeeah*]
draft	tratta [*trahttah*]
economy	economia [*aykohnohmeeah*]
(to) earn	guadagnare [*gwadahnyahray*]
earnest money	caparra [*kahpahrrah*]
earnings	guadagno [*gwadahnyoh*]
endorsement	girata [*jeerahtah*]
(to) employ	impiegare [*eempeeaygahray*]
employee	impiegato [*eempeeaygahtoh*]
employment	impiego [*eempeeaygoh*]
(to) estimate	stimare [*steemahray*]
exhibition	esposizione [*esspohzeetseeohnay*]
expense	spesa [*spayzah*]
expensive	costoso [*kohstohsoh*]
(to) export	esportare [*essporrtahray*]
export licence	licenza di esportazione [*leechentsah dee essporrtahtseeohnay*]
export duty	dazio di esportazione [*dahtseeoh dee essporrtahtseeohnay*]
factory	fabbrica [*fahbbreekah*]
favour	favore [*fahvohray*]
favourable	favorevole [*fahvohrayvohlay*]
firm	ditta [*deettah*]
fixed price	prezzo fisso [*pretsoh feesssoh*]
foreign trade	commercio estero [*kommehrchoh esstayroh*]
forwarding	spedizione [*spaydeetseeohnay*]
forwarding agent	spedizioniere [*spaydeetseeohneeayray*]
forwarding charges	spese di spedizione [*spayzay dee spaydeetseeohnay*]
free of charge	franco di spesa [*frahnkoh dee spayzah*]
(to) go bankrupt	fallire [*fahlleeray*]
goods	merce [*mehrchay*]
(to) guarantee	garantire [*gahrahnteeray*]
guarantee	garanzia [*gahrahntseeah*]
hand-made	fatto a mano [*fahttoh ah mahnoh*]
(to) import	importare [*eemporrtahray*]
import	importazione [*eemporrtahtseeohnay*]
in account	in acconto [*een ahkkontoh*]

in advance	in anticipo [*een ahnteecheepoh*]
income	entrata [*entrahtah*]
(to) increase	aumentare [*awmentahray*]
increase	aumento [*owmentoh*]
indemnity	risarcimento [*reesahrcheementoh*]
industry	industria [*eendoostreeah*]
(to) insure	assicurarsi [*ahsseekoorahrsee*]
insurance	assicurazione [*ahsseekoorahtseeohnay*]
insurance against fire	assicurazione contro incendi [*ahsseekoorahtseeohnay kontroh eenchayndee*]
insurance agaist theft	assicurazione contro il furto [*ahsseekoorahtseeohnay kontroh eel foortoh*]
insurance company	compagnia di assicurazioni [*kompahnyah dee ahsseekoorahtseeonay*]
(to) invest	investire [*ennvessteeray*]
invoice	fattura [*fahttoorah*]
item	articolo [*ahrteekohloh*]
lease	contratto d'affitto [*kontrahttoh dahffeetoh*]
(to) lend	prestare [*presstahray*]
letter of credit	lettera di credito [*layttayrah dee kraydeetoh*]
liabilities	(bilancio) passivo [*beelahnchoh pahsseevoh*]
life insurance	assicurazione sulla vita [*ahsseekoorahtseeohnay soollah veetah*]
(to) load	caricare [*kahreekahray*]
load	carico [*kahreekoh*]
loan	prestito [*pressteetoh*]
(to) lose	perdere [*pehrdayray*]
loss	perdita [*pehrdeetah*]
machine-made	fatto a macchina [*fahttoh ah mahkkeenah*]
management	direzione [*deeraytseeohnay*]
managing director	consigliere delegato [*konseelyayray daylaygahtoh*]
(to) manufacture	fabbricare [*fahbbreekahray*]
maturity	scadenza [*skahdentsah*]
merchant	commerciante [*kommehrchahntay*]
money	denaro [*daynahroh*]
occasion	occasione [*ockkahzeeohnay*]
offer	offerta [*offfehrtah*]
(to) order	ordinare [*orrdeenahray*]
order	ordinazione [*orrdeenahtseeohnay*]
out of stock	esaurito [*ayzowreetoh*]
owner	proprietario [*prohpreeaytahreeoh*]
ownership	proprietà [*prohpreeaytah*]
(to) pack	imballare [*eembahllahray*]
packing	imballaggio [*eembahllahdjoh*]
parcel	pacco [*pahkkoh*]

parcel post	pacco postale [*pahkkoh posstahlay*]
(to) patent	brevettare [*brayvettahray*]
pattern	campione [*kahmpeeohnay*]
(to) pay	pagare [*pahgahray*]
(to) pay by cash	pagare per contanti [*pahgahray pehr kontahntee*]
(to) pay by instalments	pagare a rate [*pahgahray ah rahtay*]
(to) pay for damages	risarcire [*reesahrcheeray*]
(to) pay on delivery	pagare contro assegno [*pahgahray kontroh ahssaynyoh*]
payment	pagamento [*pahgahmentoh*]
(to) pay up	versare [*vehrsahray*]
photocopy	fotocopia [*fohtohkohpeeah*]
postal order	vaglia [*vahlyah*]
price	prezzo [*pretsoh*]
price-list	listino prezzi [*leesteenoh pretsee*]
proceeds	ricavo [*reekahvoh*]
(to) produce	produrre [*prohdoorray*]
product	prodotto [*prohdottoh*]
production	produzione [*prohdootseeohnay*]
profitable	vantaggioso [*vahntahdjohsoh*]
promissory note	pagherò [*pahgayroh*]
protest	protesto [*prohtesstoh*]
(to) purchase	acquistare [*ahkkweestahray*]
receipt	ricevuta [*reechayvootah*]
remittance	rimessa di denaro [*reemesssah dee daynahroh*]
(to) request	richiedere [*reekeeaydayray*]
request	richiesta [*reekeeesstah*]
retail trade	commercio al minuto [*kommehrchoh ahl meenootoh*]
retailer	rivenditore [*reevendeetohray*]
right	diritto [*deereettoh*]
royalties	diritti d'autore [*deereettee dowtohray*]
salary	stipendio [*steependeeoh*]
sale	vendita [*vendeetah*]
sale price	prezzo di vendita [*pretsoh dee vendeetah*]
sample	campione [*kahmpeeohnay*]
sample-book	campionario [*kahmpeeohnahreeoh*]
sample fair	fiera campionaria [*feeayrah kahmpeeohnahreeah*]
(to) sell	vendere [*vendayray*]
seller	venditore [*vendeetohray*]
(to) sell by retail	rivendere [*reevendayray*]
(to) sell off	smerciare [*smehrchahray*]
selling off	smercio [*smehrchoh*]
sender	mittente [*meettentay*]
(to) ship	spedire [*spaydeeray*]
shop	negozio [*naygohtseeoh*]
(to) sign	firmare [*feermahray*]

signature	firma [*feermah*]
sold out	esaurito [*ayzowreetoh*]
specimen	esemplare [*ayzemplahray*]
(to) spend	spendere [*spendayray*]
staff	personale [*pehrsohnahlay*]
stock	scorte [*skorrtay*]
store-house	magazzino [*mahgahdzeenoh*]
(to) supply	fornire [*forrneeray*]
supply	rifornimento [*reeforneemayntoh*]
surety	mallevadore [*mahllayvahdohray*]
(to) tax	tassare [*tahssahray*]
tax	tassa [*tahssah*]
(to) trade	commerciare [*kommehrchahray*]
tradesman	negoziante [*naygohtseeahntay*]
(to) transfer	cedere [*chaydayray*]
(to) transact	trattare [*trahttahray*]
transaction	trattativa [*trahttahteevah*]
(to) transport	trasportare [*trahsporrtahray*]
traveller	viaggiatore [*veeahdjahtohray*]
(to) undersale	svendere [*sveyndayray*]
undersale	svendita [*svendeetah*]
unemployed	disoccupato [*deezockkoopahtoh*]
unemployment	disoccupazione [*deezockkoopahtseeohnay*]
(to) unload	scaricare [*skahreekahray*]
V.A.T.	I.V.A. [*eevah*]
visa	visto [*veestoh*]
(to) value	valutare [*vahlootahray*]
wages	salario [*sahlahreeoh*]
weight	peso [*paysoh*]
wholesale trade	commercio all'ingrosso [*kommehrchoch ahl eengrohssoh*]
winding up	liquidazione d'affari [*leekweedahtseeohnay dahffahree*]
workman	operaio [*ohpayrahyoh*]
workshop	officina [*offfeecheenah*]
(to) yield	fruttare [*froottahray*]

Here's my card	Ecco il mio biglietto da visita [*ekkoh eel meeoh beelyettoh dah veezeetah*]
Please, tell the manager that I am here	Voglia annunziarmi al direttore [*vollyah ahnnoontseeahrmee ahl deerettiohray*]
I have an appointment with...	Ho un appuntamento con... [*oh oon ahppoontahmentoh kon...*]
I'll call again later on	Ripasserò più tardi [*reepahssayroh peeoo tahrdee*]
I'll phone to fix an appointment	Telefonerò per fissare un appuntamento [*taylayfohnayroh pehr feessahray oon ahppoontahmentoh*]

When will he see me?	Quando potrà ricevermi? [*kwahndoh pohtrah reechayvayrmee?*]
Thank you, I'll wait	Grazie, attenderò [*grahtseeay ahttendayroh*]
I'm glad to meet you	Lieto di fare la sua conoscenza [*leeaytoh dee fahray lah sooah kohnohshentzah*]
Can you give me an estimate of the cost?	Può farmi un preventivo? [*poooh fahrmee oon prayventeevoh*]
I'd like to buy...	Vorrei compare... [*vorrayee komprahray...*]
Your prices are too high	I suoi prezzi sono troppo alti [*ee sooohee pretsee sohnoh troppoh ahltee*]
Could you make a discount?	Potrebbe farmi uno sconto? [*pohtrebbay fahrmee oonoh skontoh?*]
Sorry, but I'm not entitled to make discounts on the price list	Spiacente, ma non sono autorizzato a fare sconti su prezzi di listino [*speeahchentay mah nonn sohnoh owtohredzah toh ah fahray skontee soo pretsee dee leesteenoh*]
What are your conditions?	Quali sono le sue condizioni? [*kwahlee sohnoh lay sooay kondeetseeohnee?*]
I'm ready to make a special price for you	Sono pronto a farvi un prezzo di favore [*sohnoh prohntoh ah fahrvee oon pretsoh dee fahvohray*]
How do you wish payment to be made?	Come desidera ricevere il pagamento? [*kohmay dayseedayrah reechayvayray eel pahgahmentoh?*]
I'm ready to pay a deposit in advance	Sono disposto a versare una caparra [*sohnoh deespohstoh ah vehrsahray oonah kahpahrrah*]
Will you give me a receipt, please?	Mi prepari una ricevuta, per favore [*mee praypahree oonah reechayvootah pehr fahvohray*]
Can you provide me with an interpreter?	Può procurarmi un interprete? [*poooh prohkoorahrmee oon eentehrpraytay?*]
Please, will you show me...	Vorrebbe mostrarmi per favore... [*vohrraybbay mosstrahrmee pehr fahvohray...*]

BUSINESS CORRESPONDENCE

Introductory phraseology

Dear Sir, we have duly received your letter of...	Egregio Signore, abbiamo ricevuto la sua lettera del... [*aygrayjoh seenyohray, ahbbeeahmoh reechayvootoh lah sooah lettayrah dayl...*]
We are sorry to tell you that...	Ci dispiace doverle dire... [*chee deespeeahchay dohvayrlay deeray...*]

We would be glad to enter into business connections with your firm	Desideriamo entrare in relazione di affari con la sua ditta [*dayseedayreeahmoh entrahray een raylahtseeohnay dahffahree kon lah sooah deettah*]
With reference to your offer of... please let us know if...	Con riferimento alla vostra offerta del..., vi preghiamo di farci sapere... [*kon reefayreementoh ahllah vohstrah offfehrtah dayl...vee prayghееahmoh dee fahrchee sahpayray say...*]

Complimentary closes

Hoping to hear from you at your earliest convenience	In attesa di una sua cortese sollecita risposta [*een ahttaysah dee oonah sooha korrtaysay solllaycheetah reesposstah*]
Hoping to receive confirmation of your order	Sperando di ricevere conferma della sua ordinazione [*spayrahndoh dee reechayvayray konfehrmah dayllah sooah orrdeenahtseeohnay*]
I thank you in advance	La ringrazio in anticipo [*lah reengrahtseeoh een ahnteecheepoh*]
We look forward to hearing from you. Yours faithfully...	In attesa di una vostra risposta porgiamo distinti saluti [*een ahttaysah dee oonah vohstrah reesposstah porrjahmoh deesteentee sahlootee*]

AT THE POST OFFICE

Italian post offices can be recognized by the sign PT outside. They are normally open from 8.15 a.m. to 2 p.m., Monday to Friday, Saturday till 12 noon or I p.m. Stamps are also sold at tobacconist's and at some hotel desks. Letter boxes are generally red and yellow.

The telephone service in Italy is generally separated from the post office. Public phone booths in the street are yellow. The presence of a public phone in a bar or a caffè is indicated by a yellow sign outside. Public telephones are worked by inserting coins or tokens in the appropriate slot.

(to) address	indirizzare [*eendeereetzahhray*]
address	indirizzo [*eendeereetzoh*]
addressee (unknown)	destinatario (sconosciuto) [*dessteenahtahreeoh skohnohshootoh*]
air mail	posta aerea [*posstah ahayrayah*]
(to) be overweight	passare il peso [*pahssahray eel paysoh*]
cable	cablogramma [*kahblohgrahmmah*]
carriage paid	porto pagato [*pohrtoh pahgahtoh*]
charge	tariffa [*tahreeffah*]
coin box telephone	telefono a gettoni [*taylayfohnoh ah jettohnee*]
correspondence	corrispondenza [*korreespondentzah*]
counter	sportello [*sporrtellloh*]
daytime charge	tariffa diurna [*tahreeffah deeoornah*]
(to) deliver	recapitare [*raykahpeetahray*]
delilvery	recapito [*raykahpeetoh*]
destination	destinazione [*dessteenahtseeohnay*]
dialling code	prefisso interurbano [*prayfeessoh eentehroorbahnoh*]
direct dialling system	teleselezione [*taylaysaylaytseeohnay*]
directory	elenco telefonico [*aylengkoh taylayfohneekoh*]
form	modulo [*mohdooloh*]
head post office	posta centrale [*pohsstah chentrahlay*]
insured letter	lettera assicurata [*laytttayrah assseekoorahtah*]
international code	prefisso internazionale [*prayfeessoh eentehrnahtseeohnahlay*]
international money order	vaglia internazionale [*vahlyah eentehrnahtseeohnahlay*]
letter	lettera [*laytttayrah*]
local, long distance-call	comunicazione urbana, interurbana [*kohmooneekahtseeohnay oorbahnah, eenteroorbahnah*]
mail-box	buca per le lettere [*bookah pehr lay layttayray*]

money order	vaglia postale [*vahlyah posstahlay*]
night charge	tariffa notturna [*tahreefffah nohtttoornah*]
parcel post	pacco postale [*pahkkoh posstahlay*]
phone call	telefonata [*taylayfonahtah*]
phonogram	fonogramma [*fohnohgrammah*]
(to) post	imbucare [*eembookahray*]
postcard	cartolina [*kahrtohleenah*]
postage	tariffa [*tahreefffah*]
post-free	franchigia [*frahnkeejah*]
postman	postino [*pohsteenoh*]
postal order	assegno postale [*ahssaynyoh posstahlay*]
post-office account	conto corrente postale [*kohntoh korrayntay posstahlay*]
post-office box	casella postale [*kahselllah posstahlay*]
poste restante	fermo posta [*fayrmoh posstah*]
printed matter	stampe [*stahmpay*]
receipt	ricevuta [*reechayvootah*]
registered letter	raccomandata [*rahkkohmahndahtah*]
reservation	prenotazione [*praynohtahtseeohnay*]
return receipt requested	con ricevuta di ritorno [*kon reechayvootah dee reetorrnoh*]
reversed charge call	telefonata con tassa a carico del destinatario [*taylayfohnahtah kon tahsssah ah kahreekoh dell daysteenahtahreeoh*]
sample without value	campione senza valore [*kahmpeeohnay sentsah vahlohray*]
(to) send back	respingere [*resspeenjayray*]
sender	mittente [*meettentay*]
signature	firma [*feermah*]
special delivery	espresso [*esspresssoh*]
(to) stamp	affrancare [*ahffrahnkahray*]
stamp	francobollo [*frahnkohbollloh*]
switchboard	centralino [*chentrahleenoh*]
tax	tassa [*tahsssah*]
telegram	telegramma [*taylaygrammah*]
telegram with reply paid	telegramma con risposta pagata [*taylaygrammah kon reesposstah pahgahtah*]
(to) telegraph	telegrafare [*taylaygrahfahray*]
(to) telephone	telefonare [*taylayfohnahray*]
telephone (set)	apparecchio telefonico [*ahppahreckkeeoh taylayfohneekoh*]
telephone box	cabina telefonica [*kahbeenah taylayfohneekah*]
telephone exchange	centralino [*chentrahleenoh*]
telephone number	numero [*noomayroh*]
time collection	ora di levata [*ohrah dee layvahtah*]
urgent telegram	telegramma urgente [*taylaygrammah oorjentay*]
(to) weigh	pesare [*paysahray*]

A stamp for a letter abroad, please	Un francobollo per una lettera all'estero [*oon frahnkohbollloh pehr oonah layttayrah ahllesstayroh*]
What's the postage for a letter to London?	Qual è l'affrancatura per una lettera per Londra? [*kwahlay lahffrahngkahtoorah pehr oonah layttayrah pehr lohndrah*?]
Up to what weight can I send by sample post?	Fino a che peso posso spedire campioni senza valore? [*feenoh ah kay paysoh posssoh spaydeeray kahmpeeohnee sentsah vahlohray*?]
At which counter can I cash an international money order?	A quale sportello posso incassare un vaglia internazionale? [*ah kwahlay sporrtelloh posssoh eenkahssahray oon vahlyah eentehrnahtseeohnahlay*?]
Where's the poste restante?	Dov'è il fermo posta? [*dohvay eel fayrmoh posstah*?]
Write name and address of the sender	Scriva nome e indirizzo del mittente [*skreevah nohmay ay eendeereetzoh dell meettentay*]
Please, send an international money order to the following address	Per favore mandi un vaglia postale internazionale al seguente indirizzo [*pehr fahvohray mahndee oon vahlyah posstahlay eentehrnahtseeohnahlay ahl saygweentay eendeereetzoh*]
I want to send this parcel by registered mail	Desidero spedire questo pacco per posta raccomandata [*dayseedayroh spaydeeray kwesstoh pahkkoh pehr posstah rahkkohmahndahtah*]

TELEGRAMS

> Telegrams can be sent directly from the post office or can be dictated on the phone.

Where's the telegram counter?	Dov'è lo sportello dei telegrammi? [*dohvay loh sporrtellloh dayee taylaygrahmmee*?]
I want to send a telegram to London	Desidero mandare un telegramma a Londra [*dayseedayroh mahndahray oon taylaygrahmmah ah lohndrah*]
Can I have a form?	Posso avere un modulo? [*posssoh ahvayray oon mohdooloh*?]
How much is it per word?	Quanto costa ogni parola? [*kwahntoh kohstah ohnyee pahrohlah*?]
Can you tell me the postcode for Rome?	Può dirmi il codice postale di Roma? [*poooh deermee eel kohdeeyechay posstahlay dee rohmah*?]
How much?	Quanto le devo? [*kwahntoh lay dayvoh*?]

TELEPHONE

I want a telephone token	Desidero un gettone telefonico [*dayseedayroh oon jettohnay taylayfohneekoh*]
Can I have a telephone directory of Milan?	Posso avere l'elenco telefonico di Milano? [*posssoh ahvayray laylengkoh taylayfohneekoh dee meelahnoh*?]
What's the dialling code for Rome?	Qual è il prefisso di Roma? [*kwahlay eel prayfeessoh dee rohmah*?]
How do I get international operator?	Come si ottiene il centralino internazionale? [*kohmay see otteeaynay eel chentrahleenoh eenternahtseeohnahlay*?]
Operator, we were cut off	Centralinista, la comunicazione si è interrotta [*chentrahleeneestah, lah kohmooneekahtseeohnay see ay eentehrrohttah*]
I want to place a reversed charge call	Desidero fare una telefonata a carico del destinatario [*dayseedayroh fahray oonah taylayfohnahtah ah kahreekoh dell dessteenahtahreeoh*]
Call me this number, please	Mi chiami questo numero, per favore [*mee keeahmee kwesstoh noomayroh, pehr fahvohray*]
I want to fix an appointment for a telephone conversation	Desidero fissare un appuntamento telefonico [*dayseedayroh feessahray oon ahppoontahmentoh taylayfohneekoh*]
I'd like to make a long-distance call to...	Vorrei fare una telefonata interurbana a... [*vorrayee fahray oonah taylayfohnahtah eentehroorbahnah ah*...]
Hallo, this is... Who's speaking please?	Pronto sono... Con chi parlo? [*prontoh sohnoh... kon kee pahrloh*?]
Speak a bit louder/a bit slower, please	Parli un po' più forte/un po' più piano per favore [*pahrlee oon poh peeoo forrtay/oon poh peeoo peeahnoh pehr fahvohray*]
I want to speak to...	Desidero parlare a... [*dayseedayroh pahrlahray ah*...]
Would you please take a message?	Per favore può trasmettere un messaggio? [*pehr fahvohray poooh trahsmettayray oon messsahdjoh*?]
The phone is out of order	Il telefono non funziona [*eel taylayfonoh nonn foontseeohnah*]
What number are you calling?	Che numero chiama? [*kay noomayroh keeahmah*?]
You've got the wrong number	Chiama il numero sbagliato [*keeahmah eel noomayroh sbahlyahtoh*]
Just a moment	Un momento [*oon mohmayntoh*]

Hold on, please	Resti in linea [*resstee een leenayah*]
The line's engaged	La linea è occupata [*lah leenayah ay ockkoopahtah*]
I don't understand the name, can you spell it please?	Non capisco il nome, me lo compiti per favore [*nonn kahpeeskoh eel nohmay, may loh kohmpeetee pehr fahvohray*]

HOW TO SPELL LETTERS IN ITALIAN

English	Italian
A - B - C - D	A - B - C - D [*ah - bee - chee - dee*]
E - F - G - H	E - F - G - H [*ay - affay - jee - ahkkah*]
I - J - K - L	I - J - K - L [*ee - jay - kahppah - elllay*]
M - N - O - P	M - N - O - P [*emmay - ennay - oh - pee*]
Q - R - S - T	Q - R - S - T [*qoo - errray - esssay - tee*]
U - V - W	U - V - W [*oo-vee - dohppeeoh voo*]
X - Y - Z	X - Y - Z [*eecs - eepseelon - zaytah*]

POLICE

In Italy there are various types of police, each dealing with a different area of the law. The Carabinieri report to the Ministry of Defence and tend to deal with more serious crimes. The Polizia is a civil force which deals with crime and administrative matters. In towns, traffic is controlled by the Vigili Urbani who can also deal with less serious criminal offences. Outside the towns, the roads are patrolled by the Polizia stradale.

Emergency telephone numbers: POLICE 113
ROAD ASSISTANCE 116

abduction	rapimento [*rahpeemayntoh*]
armed robbery	rapina a mano armata [*rahpeenah ah mahnoh ahrmahtah*]
(to) arrest	arrestare [*ahrresstahray*]
bail	cauzione [*kowtseeohnay*]
bag-snatching	scippo [*sheepppoh*]
(to) call the police	chiamare la polizia [*keeahmahray lah pohleetseeah*]
car number	targa [*tahrgah*]
(to) charge	denunciare [*daynoonchahray*]
chief inspector	commissario di polizia [*kommeessahreeoh dee pohleetseeah*]
documents	documenti [*dohkoomentee*]
drunk and disorderly	ubriachezza molesta [*oobreeahketzah mohlesstah*]
expulsion order	foglio di via [*follyoh dee veeah*]
fine	contravvenzione [*kontrahvventseeohnay*]
fireman	vigile del fuoco [*veejeelay dell fooohkoh*]
fraudolent	doloso [*dohlohsoh*]
green card	carta verde [*kahrtah vehrday*]
identification papers	documenti di identificazione [*dohkoomehntee dee eedentteefeekahtseeohnay*]
infraction	infrazione [*eenfrahtseeohnay*]
insurance certificate	certificato di assicurazione [*chehrteefeekahtoh dee ahsseekoorahtseeohnay*]
lawyer	avvocato [*ahvvohkahtoh*]
(to) molest	molestare [*mohlesstahray*]
murder	omicidio [*ohmeecheedeeoh*]
police raid	retata [*raytahtah*]
prison	prigione [*preejohnay*]
provisional arrest	fermo di polizia [*fehrmoh dee pohleetseeah*]
resistance to the police	resistenza alla forza pubblica [*rayseestayntsah ahllah forrtzah poobbleekah*]

robbery	rapina [*rahpeenah*]
rowdiness at night	schiamazzi notturni [*skeeahmahtsee nottoornee*]
report	verbale [*vayrbahlay*]
rape	stupro [*stooproh*]
smuggling	contrabbando [*kontrahbbahndoh*]
theft	furto [*foortoh*]
traffic warden	vigile urbano [*veejeelay oorbahnoh*]
wanted	ricercato [*reechayrkahtoh*]

Where is the police station?	Dov'è il commissariato? [*dovay eel kommeessahreeahtoh?*]
I have been robbed	Sono stato derubato [*sohnoh stahtoh dehroobahtoh*]
My car has been broken into	Mi hanno aperto la macchina [*mee ahnnoh ahpayrtoh lah mahkkeenah*]
How much is the fine?	Quant'è la multa? [*kwantay lah mooltah?*]
I'd like to call the police	Vorrei chiamare la polizia [*vorrayee keeahmahray lah pohleetseeah*]

Viii ACCOMMODATION

If you haven't booked in advance, you can get advice from a Provincial Tourist Board (Ente Provinciale Turismo) in any of the 95 provincial capitals, or from a Local Tourist Board (Azienda Autonoma di Soggiorno), of which there are over 400 in tourist resorts.

HOTELS

LIST OF HOTELS

five star hotel	albergo di lusso [*ahlbayrgoh dee loossoh*]
first class hotel	albergo di prima categoria [*ahlbayrgoh dee preemah kahtaygohreeah*]
second class hotel	albergo di seconda categoria [*ahlbayrgoh dee saykondah kahtaygohreeah*]
third class hotel	albergo di terza categoria [*ahlbayrgoh dee tehrtsah kahtaygohreeah*]
youth hostel	ostello della gioventù [*ostaylloh dellah johventoo*]
motel	motel
boarding house	pensione [*penseeohnay*]
country inn	locanda [*lohkahndah*]
furnished rooms	camere ammobiliate [*kahmayray ahmmohbeeleeahtay*]

armchair	poltrona [*pohltrohnah*]
bath	bagno [*bahnyoh*]
bed	letto [*leyttoh*]
bed and breakfast	con sola prima colazione [*kon sohlah preemah kohlahtseeohnay*]
bell	campanello [*kahmpahnelloh*]
bill	conto [*kohntoh*]
blanket	coperta [*kohpayrtah*]
breakfast	colazione del mattino [*kohlatseeohnay dell mahtteenoh*]
case	valigia [*vahleejah*]
chair	sedia [*saydeeah*]
chamber maid	cameriera per servizio di camera [*kahmayreeayrah pehr sehrveetseeoh dee kahmayrah*]
closing time	orario di chiusura [*ohrahreeoh dee keeoosoorah*]

conference room	sala convegni [*sahlah konvaynyee*]
cook	cuoco [*kooohkoh*]
(to) deposit in safe	depositare in cassaforte [*daypohzeetahray een kahssahfohrtay*]
dining room	sala da pranzo [*sahlah dah prahntsoh*]
dirty	sporco [*sporrkoh*]
door	porta [*pohrtah*]
double bed	letto matrimoniale [*lettoh mahtreemohneeahlay*]
fan	ventilatore [*venteelahtohray*]
floor	piano [*peeahnoh*]
full board	pensione completa [*paynseeohnay kohmplaytah*]
half board	mezza pensione [*medzah paynseeohnay*]
hall porter	portiere [*porrteeayray*]
heating	riscaldamento [*reeskahldahmentoh*]
ice-cubes	cubetti di ghiaccio [*koobettee dee gheeahchchoh*]
(to) iron	stirare [*steerahray*]
key	chiave [*keeahvay*]
lamp	lampada [*lahmpahdah*]
lift	ascensore [*ahshensohray*]
light	luce [*loochay*]
linen	biancheria [*beeahngkayreeah*]
laundry service	servizio di lavanderia [*sehrveetseeoh dee lahvahndayreeah*]
maid	cameriera (di camera) [*kahmayreeayrah dee kahmayrah*]
maitre	capo cameriere [*kahpoh kahmayreeayray*]
manager	direttore [*deerettohray*]
meal time	orario dei pasti [*ohrahreeoh dayee pahstee*]
needle and thread	ago e filo [*ahgoh ay feeloh*]
night bell	campanello notturno [*kahmpahnellloh nottoornoh*]
night porter	portiere di notte [*porrteeayray dee nottay*]
page boy	fattorino [*fahttohreenoh*]
plug	spina [*speenah*]
porter	facchino [*fahkkeenoh*]
reading lamp	lampada [*lahmpahdah*]
reception	portineria [*porrteenayreeah*]
receptionist	portiere [*porrteeayray*]
room	camera [*khamayrah*]
room with/without bathroom	camera con/senza bagno [*kahmayrah kon/sentsah bahnyoh*]
room with shower	camera con doccia [*kahmayrah kon dohchchah*]
room which looks onto the garden/onto the road	stanza che dia sul giardino/sulla strada [*stahntsah kay deeah sool jahrdeenoh/soollah strahdah*]

room with a child's bed	stanza con un lettino [*stahntsah kon oon letteenoh*]
room service	servizio nella stanza [*sehrveetseeoh nellah stahntsah*]
running water	acqua corrente [*ahkkwah korrentay*]
service	servizio [*sehrveetseeoh*]
sheet	lenzuolo [*lentzooohloh*]
shutter	imposta [*eempohstah*]
soap	sapone [*sahpohnay*]
switch	interruttore [*eentehrroottohray*]
switchboard operator	centralinista [*chentrahleeneestah*]
television	televisione [*taylayveezeeohnay*]
towel	asciugamano [*ahshoogahmahnoh*]
view	vista [*veestah*]
voltage	voltaggio [*volltahdjoh*]
waiter/waitress	cameriere/cameriera [*kahmayreeayray/kahmayreeayrah*]
wash basin	lavabo [*lahvahboh*]
window	finestra [*feenesstrah*]

CHECKING IN

I want a single room/a double bed room	Desidero una camera a un letto/a due letti [*dayzeedayroh oonah kahmayrah ah oon lettoh/ah dooay lettee*]
Do you have any vacancies?	Avete camere libere? [*ahvaytay kahmayray leebayray*?]
I'd like a single room facing the sea for three days	Vorrei una camera singola sul mare per tre giorni [*vorrayee oonah kahmayrah seenggohlah sool mahray pehr tray jorrnee*]
I have a reservation	Ho fatto una prenotazione [*oh fahttoh oonah praynohtahtseeohnay*]
Is there a telephone in the room?	C'è il telefono nella stanza? [*chay eel taylayfohnoh nellah stahntsah*?]
Do you have a room with a better view?	Ha una camera con una vista più bella? [*ah oonah kahmayrah kon oonah veestah peeoo bellah*?]
Does the hotel have a garage?	L'albergo ha il garage? [*lahlbayrgoh ah eel garage*?]

PRICE

What's the price of this room for a week?	Qual è il prezzo di questa stanza per una settimana? [*kwahlay eel pretsoh dee kwesstah stahntsah pehr oonah setteemahnah*?]

It's very expensive. I want a cheaper one	È troppo cara. Ne desidero una più a buon mercato [*ay troppoh kahrah, nay dayseedayroh oonah peeoo ah booohn mehrkahtoh*]
That's fine. I'll take it	Va bene. La prendo [*vah baynay. lah prendoh*]
What's the price per night excluding meals?	Qual è il prezzo per una notte pasti esclusi? [*kwahlay eel pretsoh pehr oonah nottay pahstee esskloosee*?]
Does the price include breakfast and service?	Il prezzo comprende prima colazione e servizio? [*eel pretsoh komprenday preemah kohlahtseeohnay ay sehrveetseeoh*?]
Is the value-added tax (VAT) included?	È inclusa l'I.V.A.? [*ay eenkloozah leevah*?]
Is there any reduction for children?	Ci sono riduzioni per bambini? [*chee sohnoh reedootseeohnee pehr bahmbeenee*?]
Please, take my luggage into my room	Per favore mi porti il bagalio in stanza [*pehr fahvohray mee pohrtee eel bahgahlyoh een stahntsah*]
Where's the outlet for the shaver?	Dov'è la presa per il rasoio? [*dohvay lah praysah pehr eel rahsohyoh*?]
Can we have breakfast in our room?	Possiamo fare colazione in camera? [*posseeahmo fahray kohlahtseeohnay een kahmayrah*?]
I'd like to have my clothes washed	Vorrei far lavare i miei abiti [*vorrayee fahr lahvahray ee meeayee ahbeetee*]
I want to have my clothes dry-cleaned	Desidero far lavare a secco i miei abiti [*dayseedayroh fahr lahvahray ah seckkoh ee meeayee ahbeetee*]
I want to have my clothes ironed	Desidero far stirare i miei abiti [*dayseedayroh fahr steerahray ee meeayee ahbeetee*]
Will you please wake me at...?	Può svegliarmi alle...? [*poooh svaylyahrmee ahlllay...*?]
May I have an extra pillow?	Posso avere un guanciale in più [*posssoh ahvayray oon gwahnchahlay een peeoo*?]
Are there any messages for me?	Ci sono messaggi per me? [*chee sohnoh messsahdjee pehr may*?]
Is there any mail for me?	C'è posta per me? [*chay posstah pehr may*]

COMPLAINTS

I want a less noisy room	Desidero una stanza meno rumorosa [*dayseedayroh oonah stahntsah maynoh roomohrohsah*]
I don't like this room, it's too small	Non mi piace questa stanza, è troppo piccola [*nonn mee peeahchay kwesstah stahntsah ay troppoh peekkohlah*]

Do you have anything bigger?	Ha qualcosa di più grande? [*ah kwahlkohsah dee peeoo grahnday*?]
The air conditioner doesn't work	Il condizionatore d'aria non funziona [*eel kondeetseeohnahtohray dahreeah nonn foontseeohnah*]
The water tap is dripping	Il rubinetto sgocciola [*eel roobeenettoh sgohchchohlah*]
The blind is broken	La persiana è rotta [*lah pehrseeahnah ay rottah*]
My room has not been made up	La mia stanza non è stata rifatta [*lah meeah stahntsah nonn ay stahtah reefahttah*]
The wash-basin is clogged	Il lavabo è otturato [*eel lahvahboh ay ottoorahtoh*]
The bulb is burned out	La lampadina è bruciata [*lah lahmpahdeenah ay broochahtah*]

CHECKING OUT

I'm leaving tomorrow morning	Parto domani mattina [*pahrtoh dohmahnee mahtteenah*]
I want to pay my bill	Desidero pagare il conto [*dayzeedayroh pahgahray eel kohntoh*]
Have my bill ready, please	Mi prepari il conto, per favore [*mee praypahree eel kohntoh, pehr fahvohray*]
Please, call a taxi, and have my luggage brought down	Per favore, mi chiami un taxi e faccia portare giù le valigie [*pehr fahvohray, mee keeahmee oon taxi ay fahchchah porrtahr joo lay vahleejay*]
Is everything included?	È tutto incluso? [*ay toottoh eenkloozoh*?]
Can I pay by credit card?	Posso pagare con la carta di credito? [*posssoh pahgahray kon lah kahrtah dee kraydeeto*?]

TIPPING

Service charge is generally included in hotel bills, but if the service has been especially good, an extra tip is appropriate and appreciated. You are expected to leave a tip of 10%.

CAMPING

bottle-opener	apribottiglia [*ahpreebotteelyah*]
(to) break the camp	togliere il campeggio [*tollyayray eel kahmpaydjoh*]
butane gas	gas butano [*gahs bootahnoh*]
camp bed	branda [*brahndah*]
campground	campeggio [*kahmpaydjoh*]
campsite	campeggio [*kahmpaydjoh*]
caravan	roulotte [*rooloht*]
compass	bussola [*boossohlah*]
corkscrew	cavatappi [*kahvahtahppee*]
equipment	equipaggiamento [*aykweepahdjahmentoh*]
fare for a car	prezzo per auto [*pretsoh pehr owtoh*]
fare for a person	prezzo per persona [*pretsoh pehr pehrsohnah*]
fare for a tent	prezzo per tenda [*pretsoh pehr tendah*]
first-aid kit	cassetta di pronto soccorso [*kahssettah dee prontoh sockkorrsoh*]
flashlight	lampada tascabile [*lahmpahdah tahskahbeelay*]
gas camp stove	fornello a gas [*fohrnellloh ah gahs*]
gas cartridges	cartucce di gas [*kahrtoocchay dee gahs*]
gas lamp	lampada a gas [*lampahdah ah gahs*]
groundsheet	telo per il terreno [*tayloh pehr eel tehrraynoh*]
hammer	martello [*mahrtellloh*]
hammock	amaca [*ahmahkah*]
inflatable mattress	materasso gonfiabile [*mahtayrahssoh gonfeeahbeelay*]
knapsack	zaino [*dsaheenoh*]
mat	stuoia [*stooohyah*]
methylated spirits	alcool metilico [*ahlkohohl mayteeleekoh*]
mosquito net	zanzariera [*dsahndsahreeayrah*]
one-place-pup tent	tenda canadese a un posto [*tayndah kahnahdaysay ah oon pohstoh*]
pickets	picchetti [*peekkayttee*]
(to) pitch a tent	piantare una tenda [*peeahntahray oonah tayndah*]
rope	corda [*korrdah*]
rucksack	zaino [*dsaheenoh*]
screwdriver	cacciavite [*kahchchahveetay*]
sleeping bag	sacco a pelo [*sahkkoh ah payloh*]
tent	tenda [*tayndah*]
tent pegs	picchetti per tenda [*peekkayttee pehr tayndah*]
tent pole	palo per tenda [*pahloh pehr tayndah*]
tent trailer	carrello-tenda [*kahrrellloh tayndah*]
ties	tiranti [*teerahntee*]
torch	pila [*peelah*]

two-places-pup tent	tenda canadese a due posti [*tayndah kahnahdaysay ah dooay pohstee*]
vacuum flask	thermos [*tayrmohs*]
Is there a campsite nearby?	C'è un campeggio nelle vicinanze? [*chay oon kahmpaydjoh nelllay veecheenahntzay*?]
Can we pitch our tent here?	Possiamo piantare la tenda qui? [*possseeahmoh peeahntahray lah tayndah kwee*?]
What's the fare for a tent?	Qual è il prezzo per una tenda? [*kwahlay eel pretsoh pehr oonah tayndah*?]
What's the charge per day?	Quanto si paga al giorno? [*kwahntoh see pahgah ahl jorrnoh*?]
Is there room for a caravan?	C'è spazio per una roulotte? [*chay spahtseeoh pehr oonah roolot*?]
Is there electricity?	C'è l'elettricità? [*chay laylettreecheetah*?]
Where are the toilets?	Dove sono i gabinetti? [*dohvay sohnoh ee gahbeenettee*?]
Where can I get camping equipment?	Dove posso trovare materiale per campeggio? [*dohvay pohsssoh trohvahray mahtayreeahlay pehr kahmpaydjoh*?]
When will you break camp?	Quando toglierete il campo? [*kwahndoh tollyayraytay eel kahmpoh*?]
Is the tourist tax included?	È compresa la tassa di soggiorno? [*ay kompraysah lah tahssah dee sohdjorrnoh*?]
Do you have any vacancies?	Avete dei posti liberi? [*ahvaytay dayee pohstee leebayree*?]

Campsites are plentiful and generally well-maintained. Discounts are available for campers holding the International Camping Carnet. Never camp without permission in fields or in common land, as penalties are severe.

iX EATING OUT

PLACES WHERE MEALS AND DRINKS ARE SERVED

restaurant	ristorante [*reestohrahntay*]
snack-bar	tavola calda [*tahvohlah kahldah*]
fast-food place	fast-food
pizzeria	pizzeria [*peetsayreeah*]
café	caffè [*kahffay*]
ice-cream parlour	gelateria [*jaylahtayreeah*]
inn	osteria [*ohstayreeah*]
takeaway, cook-shop	rosticceria [*rossteechchayreeah*]
cheap restaurant	trattoria [*trahttohreeah*]

MEALS AND LAID TABLE

breakfast	prima colazione [*preemah kohlahtseeohnay*]
dinner	pranzo [*prahntsoh*]
lunch	colazione [*kohlahtseeohnay*]
supper	cena [*chaynah*]
bottle	bottiglia [*botteelyah*]
breadsticks	grissini [*greessseenee*]
carafe	caraffa [*kahrafffah*]
chair	sedia [*saydeeah*]
corkscrew	cavatappi [*kahvahtahppee*]
cruet-stand	oliera [*ohleeayrah*]
cup	tazza [*tahtsah*]
fork	forchetta [*forrkettah*]
glass	bicchiere [*beekkeeayray*]
knife	coltello [*kolltellloh*]
napkin	tovagliolo [*tohvahlyohloh*]
nut-cracker	schiaccianoci [*skeeahchchahnohchee*]
plate	piatto [*peeahttoh*]
salt-cellar	saliera [*sahleeayrah*]
spoon	cucchiaio [*kookkeeahyoh*]
sugar bowl	zuccheriera [*tsookkayreeayrah*]
table cloth	tovaglia [*tohvahlyah*]
talcum powder	borotalco [*bohrohtahlkoh*]
tea-cup	tazza da tè [*tahtsah dah tay*]
tea-spoon	cucchiaino [*kookkeeaheenoh*]
tooth-pick	stuzzicadenti [*stootseekahdentee*]
tray	vassoio [*vahssohyoh*]

AT THE RESTAURANT

STAFF

cook	cuoco [*koooohkoh*]
maitre d'hotel	maitre d'hotel
head-waiter	capocameriere [*kahpohkahmayreeayray*]
waiter	cameriere [*kahmayreeayray*]
waitress	cameriera [*kahmayreeayrah*]

MENU

Appetizers

anchovies	acciughe [*ahchchooghay*]
artichokes	carciofi [*kahrchohfee*]
assorted hors d'oeuvre	antipasto misto [*ahnteepahstoh meestoh*]
Bologna sausage	mortadella [*morrtahdayllah*]
caviar	caviale [*kahveeahlay*]
cold cuts of pork	affettati misti [*ahfffayttiahtee meestee*]
corned tongue with jelly	lingua salmistrata con gelatina [*leenggwah sahlmeestrahtah kon jaylahteenah*]
cured ham from Parma	prosciutto crudo di Parma [*prohshoottoh kroodoh dee pahrmah*]
ham	prosciutto [*prohshoottoh*]
ham with melon	prosciutto con melone [*prohshoottoh kon maylohnay*]
mozzarella cheese with tomatoes	mozzarella con pomodori [*motzahrayllah kon pohmohdohree*]
olives	olive [*ohleevay*]
oysters	ostriche [*osstreekay*]
paté	paté di fegato [*pahtay dee faygahtoh*]
pickles	sottaceti [*sohtttahchaytee*]
Russian salad	insalata russa [*eensahlahtah roossah*]
salami	salame [*sahlahmay*]
sardines in oil	sardine all'olio [*sahrdeenay ahll ohleeoh*]
sea-food hors d'oeuvre	antipasto di frutti di mare [*ahnteepahstoh dee froottee dee mahray*]
smoked salmon	salmone affumicato [*sahlmohnay ahffoomeekhatoh*]
tunny in oil	tonno [*tohnnoh*]

First course

bean soup	minestra di fagioli [*meenesstrah dee fahjohlee*]
chicken soup	brodo di pollo [*brohdoh dee pollloh*]

meat soup	brodo di carne [*brohdoh dee kahrnay*]
small pasta in chicken soup	pastina in brodo [*pahsteenah een brohdoh*]
pea soup	minestra di piselli [*meenesstrah dee peezellee*]
potato "gnocchi"	gnocchi di patate [*nyockkee dee pahtahtay*]
rice and vegetable soup	minestrone [*meenaystrohnay*]
risotto	risotto [*reesohtttoh*]
spaghetti[1] with tomato sauce	spaghetti al sugo [*spahgaytttee ahl soogoh*]
spaghetti with meat sauce	spaghetti al ragù [*spahgaytttee ahl rahgoo*]
vegetable soup	minestra di verdura [*meenaystrah dee vehrdoorah*]

> The well-known "spaghetti" should be eaten by selecting a few strands with the fork, and twisting the latter in one's hand until the lengths of spaghetti are neatly wound round the prongs.

Meat

chop	braciola [*brahchohlah*]
cutlet	cotoletta [*kohtohlaytttah*]
escalope	scaloppina [*skahlohpppeenah*]
fillet	filetto [*feelettoh*]
liver	fegato [*faygahtoh*]
marrow-bone	ossobuco [*osssohbookoh*]
meatballs	polpette [*pohlpaytttay*]
pie	pasticcio [*pahsteechchoh*]
pig's trotter	zampone [*tsahmpohnay*]
roast	arrosto [*ahrrosstoh*]
rolled veal fillets	involtini [*eenvollteenee*]
sausage	salsiccia [*sahlseechchah*]
steak	bistecca [*beesteckkah*]
meat stew	spezzatino [*spetsahteenoh*]
veal with tunny sauce	vitello tonnato [*veetaylllloh tohnnahtoh*]
tongue	lingua [*leenggwah*]
tripe	trippa [*treepppah*]

Game and poultry

boiled chicken	pollo lesso [*pollloh lesssoh*]
capon	cappone [*kahppohnay*]
chicken	galletto [*gahlllaytttoh*]
duck	anatra [*ahnahtrah*]
guinea fowl	faraona [*fahrahohnah*]
kid goat	capretto [*kahpraytttoh*]

pheasant	fagiano [*fahjahnoh*]
quails	quaglie [*kwahlyeeay*]
rabbit	coniglio [*kohneelyoh*]
roast chicken	pollo arrosto [*pollloh ahrrosstoh*]
salmi hare	lepre in salmì [*laypray een sahlmee*]
turkey	tacchino [*tahkkeenoh*]
wild boar	cinghiale [*cheenggheeahlay*]

Fish and seafood

anchovies	acciughe [*ahchchooghay*]
bass	branzino [*brahntzeenoh*]
clams	vongole [*vonggohlay*]
cod	merluzzo [*mehrlootzoh*]
crayfish	gamberi [*gahmbayree*]
cuttlefish	seppia [*seppeeah*]
dogfish	palombo [*pahlohmboh*]
eel	anguilla [*ahnggweellah*]
fish-soup	zuppa di pesce [*tsooppah dee payshay*]
herring	aringa [*ahreengah*]
lobster	aragosta [*ahrahgosstah*]
mackerel	sgombro [*sgombroh*]
mixed fry	fritto misto [*freetttoh meestoh*]
mussels	cozze [*kotzay*]
octopus	polpo [*pohlpoh*]
oysters	ostriche [*osstreekay*]
plaice	orata [*ohrahtah*]
red mullet	triglia [*treelyah*]
salmon	salmone [*sahlmohnay*]
salt cod	baccalà [*bahkkahlah*]
sardine	sardina [*sahrdeenah*]
shrimps	gamberetti [*gahmbayretttee*]
sole	sogliola [*sollyohlah*]
squid	seppia [*saypppeeah*]
sturgeon	storione [*stohreeohnay*]
swordfish	pesce spada [*payshay spahdah*]
trout	trota [*trohtah*]
tunny	tonno [*tonnoh*]
whiting	nasello [*nahsellloh*]

Vegetables

artichokes	carciofi [*kahrchohfee*]
asparagus	asparagi [*ahspahrahjee*]
aubergine	melanzana [*maylahntsahnah*]
beans	fagioli [*fahjohlee*]
beetroot	barbabietola [*bahrbahbeeaytohlah*]
Brussel sprouts	cavolini di Bruxelles [*kahvohleenee dee Bruxelles*]
cabbage	cavolo [*kahvohloh*]
carrots	carote [*kahrohtay*]
cauliflower	cavolfiore [*kahvohlfeeohray*]

celery	sedano [*saydahnoh*]
cucumber	cetriolo [*chaytreeohloh*]
fennel	finocchio [*feenockkeeoh*]
green beans	fagiolini [*fahjohleenee*]
green salad	insalata verde [*eensahlahtah vayrday*]
lettuce	lattuga [*lahtttoogah*]
mashed potatoes	purè di patate [*pooray dee pahtahtay*]
mushrooms	funghi [*foonghee*]
onions	cipolle [*cheepohlllay*]
parsley	prezzemolo [*pretsaymohloh*]
peppers	peperoni [*paypayrohnee*]
potatoes	patate [*pahtahtay*]
pumpkin	zucca [*tsookkah*]
spinach	spinaci [*speenahchee*]
tomatoes	pomodori [*pohmohdohree*]
turnips	rape [*rahpay*]
truffles	tartufi [*tahrtoofee*]

Spices and herbs

basil	basilico [*bahzeeleekoh*]
bay	lauro [*lowroh*]
garlic	aglio [*ahlyoh*]
nutmeg	noce moscata [*nohchay mohskahtah*]
origan	origano [*ohreegahnoh*]
parsley	prezzemolo [*pretsaymohloh*]
rosemary	rosmarino [*rossmahreenoh*]
saffron	zafferano [*dsahffayrahnoh*]
sage	salvia [*sahlveeah*]

Egg dishes

boiled eggs	uova alla coque [*ooohvah ahllah kock*]
fried eggs	uova al tegame [*ooohvah ahl taygahmay*]
hard boiled eggs	uova sode [*ooohvah sohday*]
omelette	frittata [*freettahtah*]
poached eggs	uova in camicia [*ooohvah een kahmeechah*]
scrambled eggs	uova strapazzate [*ooohvah strahpahtsahtay*]
stuffed eggs	uova ripiene [*ooohvah reepeeaynay*]

Fruit

apple	mela [*maylah*]
apricot	albicocca [*ahlbeekockkah*]
baked fruit	frutta al forno [*froottah ahl forrnoh*]
cherry	ciliegia [*cheeleeayjah*]
cooked fruit	frutta cotta [*froottah kohttah*]
dried fruit	frutta secca [*froottah seckkah*]
fresh fruit	frutta fresca [*froottah fresskah*]

fruit salad	macedonia di frutta [*mahchaydohneeah dee froottah*]
grape-fruit	pompelmo [*pohmpaylmoh*]
grapes	uva [*oovah*]
hazelnut	nocciola [*nohchchohlah*]
melon	melone [*maylohnay*]
orange	arancia [*ahrahnchah*]
peach	pesca [*pesskah*]
pear	pera [*payrah*]
pineapple	ananas [*ahnahnahs*]
plum	prugna [*proonyah*]
raspberries	lamponi [*lahmpohnee*]
strawberries in cream	fragole alla panna [*frahgohlay ahllah pahnnah*]
tangerine	mandarino [*mahndareenoh*]
walnut	noce [*nohchay*]

Dessert

apple pie	torta di mele [*torrtah dee maylay*]
jam tart	crostata [*krohstahtah*]
ice-cream	gelato [*jaylahtoh*]
pudding	budino [*boodeenoh*]
slice of cake	fetta di torta [*fettah dee torrtah*]
trifle	zuppa inglese [*tsooppah eenglaysay*]

Can you recommend a fast food place?	Può consigliarmi un fast food? [*poooh konseelyahrmee oon fast food?*]
Are there any cheap restaurants around here?	Vi sono ristoranti economici qui vicino? [*vee sohnoh reestohrahntee aykohnohmeechee kwee veecheenoh*]
I'd like to reserve a table for 6	Vorremmo riservare un tavolo per 6 [*vohrraymmoh reesehrvahray oon tahvohloh pehr sayee*]
Could we have a table on the terrace?	Potremmo avere un tavolo sulla terrazza? [*pohtraymmoh ahvayray oon tahvohloh soolllah tehrrahtsah?*]
Waiter, may I have the menu please?	Cameriere, posso avere il menu per favore? [*kahmayreeayray, pohsssoh ahvayray eel maynoo pehr fahvohray?*]
What's on the tourist menu?	Cosa offre il menu turistico? [*kohsah ohfffray eel maynoo tooreesteekoh?*]

> A tourist menu offers a fixed-price three or four course meal with limited choice, or the speciality of the day.

What do you recommend?	Cosa ci consiglia? [*kohsah chee kohnseehlyeeah?*]
What is your speciality?	Quale è la vostra specialità? [*kwahlay ay lah vosstrah spaychahleetah?*]

I'd like a bottle of red wine and some mineral water	Vorrei una bottiglia di vino rosso e dell'acqua minerale [*vorrayee oona botteelyah dee veenoh rosssoh ay dell ahkkwah meenayrahlay*]
I'd like a grilled steak	Vorrei una bistecca alla fiorentina [*vorrayee oona beesteckkah ahllah feeohraynteenah*]
Do you like your meat rare, medium or well-done?	Vuole la carne al sangue, a puntino, ben cotta? [*vooohlay lah kahrnay ahl sahnggway, ah poonteenoh oh bayn kohttah?*]
I'd like a dessert, please	Vorrei un dessert per favore [*vorrayee oon dessert pehr fahvohray*]

> When eating out you may see on the menu "il vino della casa" (the house wine). House wines are well worth trying as they are normally cheaper than bottled wines without being of inferior quality.

THE BILL

I'd like to pay	Vorrei pagare [*vorrayee pahgahray*]
The bill, please	Il conto per favore [*eel kohntoh pehr fahvohray*]
Is everything included?	È tutto compreso? [*ay toottoh kompresoh*?]
Can I pay with this credit card?	Posso pagare con questa carta di credito? [*pohsssoh pahgahray kohn kwesstah kahrtah dee kraydeetoh*?]
Keep the change	Tenga il resto [*tayngah eel raystoh*]
Thank you, this is for you	Grazie, questo è per lei [*grahtseeay kwesstoh ay pehr layee*]

COMPLAINTS

The meat is overdone	La carne è troppo cotta [*lah kahrnay ay troppoh kohttah*]
May I change this?	Posso cambiare questo? [*posssoh kahmbeeahray kwesstoh*?]
This is too salty	Questo è troppo salato [*kwesstoh ay troppoh sahlahtoh*]
The food is cold	Il cibo è freddo [*eel cheeboh ay freddoh*]
The fish isn't fresh	Il pesce non è fresco [*eel payschay nonn ay fresskoh*]
This glass isn't clean	Questo bicchiere non è pulito [*qwesstoh beekkeeayray nonn ay pooleetoh*]
I want to speak to the Manager	Vorrei parlare col direttore [*vorrrayee pahrlahray cohl deerettohray*]

There must be some mistake in this bill	Deve esserci un errore in questo conto [*dayvay esssayrchee oon ehrrohray een kwesstoh kohntoh*]

LOCAL DISHES

Liguria

Minestrone alla genovese [*meenesstrohnay ahllah jaynohvaysay*]	**Thick vegetable soup with rice or pasta**
pesto [*paystoh*]	**A sauce made with garlic, basil, parmesan cheese, pine kernels and mixed in oil**
Trenette al pesto [*traynayttay ahl paystoh*]	**Small pieces of pasta flavoured with pesto**

Piemonte

Fonduta [*fohndootah*]	**Cream cheese with butter, eggs, milk and white truffles**
Bagna cauda [*bahnyah kahoodah*]	**Artichokes and celery served with a sauce of truffles, garlic, anchovy, butter and oil**

Lombardia

Cassola [*kahssolah*]	**A mixture of various different kinds of meat, cooked with vegetables**
Cotoletta alla milanese [*kohtohlayttah ahllah meelahnaysay*]	**Veal cutlets, which have been rolled in egg and breadcrumb and fried**
Osso buco [*osssoh bookoh*]	**A stew of veal with marrow bones, mixed vegetables and spices**
Risotto allo zafferano [*reesohttoh ahlloh dsahffayrahnoh*]	**Rice flavoured with saffron**

Veneto

Brodetto [*brohdayttoh*]	**Fish soup served with cornmeal mush** (polenta)
Baccalà mantecato [*bahkahlah mahntaykahtoh*]	**Dried cod which has been boiled and beaten up in oil**

Emilia

Tortellini [*tohrtaylleenee*]	**Rings of dough filled with seasoned minced meat and served in broth or with a sauce**
Zampone e mortadella [*dsahmpohnay ay morrtahdayllah*]	**Local pork sausages which are very highly seasoned**

Toscana

Bistecca alla fiorentina [*beesteckkah ahllah feeohraynteenah*]	**Grilled veal cutlet, seasoned with salt, pepper and lemon juice**

Lazio

Gnocchi alla romana [*nyockkee ahllah rohmahnah*]	**Baked semolina gnocchi, with milk and cheese**
Fettuccine alla romana [*fayttoochcheenay ahllah rohmahnah*]	**Egg pasta flavoured with beef gravy**

Campania

Maccheroni al ragù [*mahkkayrohnee ahl rahgoo*]	**Macaroni with ragù**
Maccheroni alla marinara [*mahkkayrohnee ahllah mahreenahrah*]	**Macaroni, with a sauce made of mussels, garlic, oil and parsley**
Parmigiana di melanzane [*pahrmeejahnah dee maylahntsahnay*]	**Parmesan cheese with aubergines**
Pizza napoletana [*peetsah nahpohlaytahnah*]	**Flat dough circles baked with cheese, anchovies, tomato sauce, etc.**

Sicilia

Pasta alle sarde [*pahstah ahllay sahrday*]	**Pasta with sardines**
Caponata [*kahpohnahtah*]	**Aubergines and celery cooked with sieved tomato, peppers and olives**

BAR

At bars coffee and drinks are served. In most of them first you have to get a ticket from the cashier. Then you go to the counter and order what you want. Several bars have tables and chairs. If you want to be served at a table, the charge for your drinks and food will be slightly higher.

camomile	camomilla [*kahmohmeellah*]
cappuccino	cappuccino [*kahppoochcheenoh*]

Cappuccino is a delicious mixture of coffee and hot milk, dusted with cocoa.

chocolate	cioccolata [*chockkohlahtah*]
coffee	caffè [*kahffay*]
coffee with cream	caffè con panna [*kahffay kohn pahnnah*]
coke	coca cola [*kohkah kohlah*]
fruit juice	succo di frutta [*sookkoh dee froottah*]
lemonade	limonata [*leemohnahtah*]
milk shake	frappè [*frahppay*]
milk with coffee	latte macchiato [*lahttay mahkkeeahtoh*]
mineral water	acqua minerale [*ahkkwah meenayrahlay*]
non-alcoholic aperitif	aperitivo analcolico [*ahpayreeteevoh ahnahlkohleekoh*]
orangeade	aranciata [*ahrahnchahtah*]
orange-juice	spremuta d'arancio [*spraymootah dahrahnchoch*]
shake	frullato [*froolllahtoh*]
tea with lemon	tè con limone [*tay kon leemohnay*]
tea with milk	tè con latte [*tay kon lahttay*]
tomato juice	succo di pomodoro [*sookkoh dee pohmohdohroh*]
tonic water	acqua tonica [*ahkkwah tohneekah*]

ALCOHOLIC DRINKS

aperitif	aperitivo [ahpayreeteevoh]
beer	birra [*beerrah*]
brandy	brandy
on draught (of beer)	alla spina [*ahllah speenah*]
sparkling white wine	spumante [*spoomahntay*]
wine	vino [*veenoh*]

Ice-creams

ice-creams	gelati [*jaylahtee*]

cornet	cono [*kohnoh*]
cup	coppa [*kohppah*]
granita	granita [*grahneetah*]
mixed ice-cream with whipped cream	gelato misto con panna montata [*jaylahtoh meestoh kon pahnnah mohntahtah*]
semifreddo	semifreddo [*saymeefrayddoh*]
I'd like a caffè espresso please	Per favore (vorrei) un caffè espresso [*pehr fahvohray oon kahffay esspresssoh*]

The Italian caffè espresso is served in demi-tasses and it is stronger than ordinary coffee.

How much is it?	Quant'è [*qwahntay?*]
Please get the ticket at the cash desk	Ritiri lo scontrino alla cassa [*reeteeree loh skontreenoh ahllah kahssah*]
Please bring me a 'cappuccino' with a brioche	Per favore, un cappuccino e una brioche [*pehr fahvohray oon kahppoochcheenoh ay oonah brioche*]
Give me a mug of dark beer please	Un boccale di birra scura, per favore [*oon bockkahlay dee beerrah skoorah, pehr fahvohray*]
Please another glass of wine and two teas with milk and without sugar	Per favore, un altro bicchiere di vino, due tè al latte senza zucchero [*pehr fahvohray oon ahltroh beekkeeayray dee veenoh ay dooay tay ahl lahttay sentsah tsookkayroh*]

WINES

Italy produces more wine than any other country and names like Frascati, Lambrusco and Chianti are known throughout the world. In Italy wine is normally drunk with meals but it is also taken as an aperitif and with desserts. All bars and cafes are licensed to sell alcohol and one can have a glass of wine or spirits at any time of the day. Osterie and enoteche (wine bars) have wine on tap and sell a huge range of Italian and foreign wines.

You'll often see the letters DOC on the label of a wine bottle: this stands for 'denominazione di origine controllata' and means that the wine has been produced with high quality grapes and that a quality control has been carried out to verify this.

X SHOPPING AND SERVICES

MAIN SHOPS

antique shop	antiquario [*ahnteekwahreeoh*]
baker's shop	panetteria [*pahnettayreeah*]
barber's shop	barbiere [*bahrbeeayray*]
bookshop	libreria [*leebrayreeah*]
butcher's shop	macelleria [*mahchaylllayreeah*]
chemist's shop	farmacia [*fahrmahcheeah*]
clothes shop	negozio d'abbigliamento [*naygotseeoh dee ahbbeelyahmentoh*]
confectioner's shop	pasticceria [*pahsteechchayreeah*]
dairy	latteria [*lahttayreeah*]
delicatessen shop	salumeria [*sahloomayreeah*]
department store	grande magazzino [*grahnday mahgahdzeenoh*]
drycleaner's	lavanderia a secco [*lahvahndayreeah ah seckkoh*]
fish-shop	pescheria [*pesskayreeah*]
florist	fioraio [*feeohraheeoh*]
furrier's shop	pellicceria [*pellleechchayreeah*]
greengrocer's shop	fruttivendolo [*froottteevehndohloh*]
grocery	negozio di alimentari, drogheria [*naygohtseeoh dee ahleementahree, drohgayreeah*]
hairdresser's shop	parrucchiere [*pahrrookkeeayray*]
hardware store	ferramenta [*fehrrahmentah*]
herbalist's shop	erboristeria [*ehrbohreestayreeah*]
jeweller's shop	gioielleria [*johyelllayreeah*]
laundry	lavanderia [*lahvahndayreeah*]
market	mercato [*mehrkahtoh*]
news agency	giornalaio [*jorrnahlahyoh*]
news-stand	edicola [*aydeekohlah*]
optician	ottico [*ohtteekoh*]
perfumery	profumeria [*prohfoomayreeah*]
photografy	articoli fotografici [*ahrteekohlee fohtohgrahfeechee*]
shoemaker's (repairs)	calzolaio [*kahltzohlahyoh*]
shoe-shop	negozio di scarpe [*naygohtseeoh dee skahrpay*]
sporting goods shop	negozio di articoli sportivi [*naygohtseeoh dee ahrteekohlee sporrteevee*]
stationer's shop	cartoleria [*kahrtohlayreeah*]
tobacconist's	tabaccheria [*tahbahkkayreeah*]
toy-shop	giocattoli [*johkahttohlee*]
watchmaker	orologiaio [*ohrohlohjahyoh*]

Where's the main shopping area?	Dov'è la principale zona di negozi? [*dohvay lah preencheepahlay dsohnah dee naygohtsee?*]
How do I get there?	Come ci arrivo? [*kohmay chee ahrreevoh?*]
Where can I find a good florist?	Dove trovo un buon fiorista? [*dohvay trohvoh oon booohn feeohreestah?*]
Can I help you?	Posso aiutarla? [*posssoh ahyootahrlah?*]
Thank you, but I'm just looking	Grazie ma do solo un'occhiata [*grahtseeay mah doh sohloh oon ockkeeahtah*]
Can you show me some...	Può mostrarmi dei... [*poooh mosstrahrmee dayee...*]
Do you have any...	Ha dei... [*ah dayee...*]
Where can I pay?	Dove posso pagare? [*dohvay posssoh pahgahray?*]
How much is it?	Quant'è [*kwahntay?*]
Do you accept credit cards?	Accettate carte di credito? [*ahchchayttahtay kahrtay dee kraydeetoh?*]
I don't understand	Non capisco [*nonn kahpeeskoh*]
I'll take it with me	Lo porto via [*loh pohrtoh veeah*]
Please send it to this address	Per favore lo mandi a questo indirizzo [*pehr fahvohray loh mahndee ah kwesstoh eendeereetzoh*]
I want to return this	Desidero rendere questo [*dayseedayroh rendayray kwesstoh*]
Here's the receipt	Ecco la ricevuta [*ekkoh lah reechayvootah*]

AT THE BAKER'S

a loaf	pagnotta [*pahnyottah*]
biscuits	biscotti [*beeskohttee*]
bran	crusca [*krooskah*]
bread	pane [*pahnay*]
bread-crumbs	pangrattato [*pahngrahtttahtoh*]
bread made with oil	pane all'olio [*pahnay ahllohleeoh*]
bread sticks	grissini [*greesseenee*]
flour	farina [*fahreenah*]
fresh bread	pane fresco [*pahnay fresskoh*]
roll	panino [*pahneenoh*]
rusks	fette biscottate [*fayttay beeskohtttahtay*]
rye bread	pane di segale [*pahnay dee saygahlay*]
wholemeal bread	pane integrale [*pahnay eentaygrahlay*]
yeast	lievito [*leeayveetoh*]

AT THE BARBER'S/AT THE HAIRDRESSER

beard	barba [*bahrbah*]
(to) bleach	ossigenare [*ossseejaynahray*]

(to) blow-dry	asciugare col fon [*ahshoogahray kohl fohn*]
(to) brush	spazzolare [*spahtsohlahray*]
brush	spazzola [*spahtsohlah*]
(to) comb	pettinare [*paytteenahray*]
(to) curl	arricciare [*ahrreechchahray*]
dandruff	forfora [*forrfohrah*]
dryer	casco [*kahskoh*]
(to) dye	tingere [*teenjayray*]
friction	frizione [*freetseeohnay*]
hair	capelli [*kahpaylllee*]
hair dye	tintura per capelli [*teentoorah pehr kahpaylllee*]
hair setting	messa in piega [*messsah een peeaygah*]
hair spray	lacca [*lahckkah*]
hair style	pettinatura [*petteenahtoorah*]
hand dryer	fon [*fohn*]
lather	schiuma [*skeeoomah*]
lotion	lozione [*lohtseeohnay*]
moustache	baffi [*bahffee*]
nail varnish	smalto per unghie [*smahltoh pehr oongheeay*]
parting	riga, scriminatura [*reegah, skreemeenahtoorah*]
permanent wave	permanente [*pehrmahnentay*]
razor	rasoio [*rahsohyoh*]
shampoo	lavatura della testa [*lahvahtoorah dellah tesstah*]
(to) shave	radere [*rahdayray*]
(to) wash the hair	lavare i capelli [*lahvahray ee kahpayllee*]
wave	ondulazione [*ondoolahtseeohnay*]

I wish to be shaved	Desidero farmi fare la barba [*dayzeedayroh fahrmee fahray lah bahrbah*]
Shave and hair-cut, please	Per favore, barba e capelli [*pehr fahvohray bahrbah ay kahpaylllee*]
I'd like to have my hair cut	Vorrei farmi tagliare i capelli [*vorrayee fahrmee tahlyahray ee kahpaylllee*]
An anti-scurf lotion, please	Per favore, una lozione anti-forfora [*pehr fahvohray, oonah lotseeohnay ahnteefohrfohrah*]
Trim my beard, please	Mi spunti la barba per favore [*mee spoontee lah bahrbah pehr fahvohray*]
When can I come for a hair-set?	Quando posso venire per una messa in piega? [*kwahndoh posssoh vayneeray pehr oonah messsah een peeaygah?*]
I want my hair washed and permed	Desidero lavarmi i capelli e fare la permanente [*dayzeedayroh lahvahrmee ee kahpaylllee ay fahray lah pehrmahnayntay*]

An anti-dandruff shompoo, please	Per favore uno shampoo antiforfora [*pehr fahvohray, oonoh shampoh ahnteefohrfohrah*]
Please cut the bang just a little	Per favore, mi tagli un po' la frangetta [*pehr fahvohray mee tahlyee oon poh lah frahnjayttah*]
How much is the dyeing?	Quant'è la tintura? [*kwahntay lah teentoorah*]
I'd like it cut and shaped	Vorrei taglio e messa in piega [*vorrayee tahlyoh ay messsah een peeaygah*]

BOOKSHOP AND NEWS AGENCY

advertisements	inserzioni [*eensayrtseeohnee*]
afternoon edition	edizione del pomeriggio [*aydeetseeohnay dell pohmayreedjoh*]
a monthly	mensile [*manseelay*]
article	articolo [*ahrteekohloh*]
a sports paper	giornale sportivo [*jorrnahlay sporrteevoh*]
autobiography	autobiografia [*owtohbeeohgrahfeeah*]
back number	arretrato [*ahrraytrahtoh*]
binding	legatura [*laygahtoorah*]
biography	biografia [*beeohgrahfeeah*]
brochure	opuscolo [*ohpooskohloh*]
book	libro [*leebroh*]
catalogue	catalogo [*kahtahlohgoh*]
collection	raccolta [*rahkkolltah*]
comic-book/comics	fumetti [*foomayttee*]
crime news	cronaca nera [*krohnahkah nayrah*]
cover	copertina [*kohpehrteenah*]
daily paper	quotidiano [*kwohteedeeahnoh*]
diary	agenda [*ahjendah*]
dictionary	vocabolario [*vohkahbohlahreeoh*]
edition out of print	edizione esaurita [*aydeetseeohnay ayzowreetah*]
encyclopaedia	enciclopedia [*encheeklohpaydeeah*]
essay	saggio [*sahdjoh*]
evening edition	edizione della sera [*aydeetseeohnay delllah sayrah*]
extra edition	edizione straordinaria [*aydeetseeohnay strahorrdeenahreeah*]
fairy tale	fiaba [*feeahbah*]
fortnightly magazine	rivista quindicinale [*reeveestah kweendeecheenahlay*]
guide book	guida [*gweedah*]
half priced book	a metà prezzo [*ah maytah praytsoh*]
illustrated book	libro illustrato [*leebroh eellloostrahtoh*]
illustrated magazine	rotocalco [*rohtohkahlkoh*]
index	indice [*eendeechay*]
instalment	dispensa [*deespaynsah*]

late night edition	edizione della notte [*aydeetseeohnay delllah nottay*]
leading article	articolo di fondo [*ahrteekohloh dee fohndoh*]
library	biblioteca [*beebleeohtaykah*]
map of the city	pianta della città [*peeahntah delllah cheettah*]
manual	manuale [*mahnooahlay*]
magazine	rivista [*reeveestah*]
morning edition	edizione del mattino [*aydeetseeohnay dell mahtteenoh*]
novel	romanzo [*rohmahntsoh*]
obituary	necrologio [*naykrohlohjeeoh*]
paperback	edizione tascabile [*aydeetseeohnay tahskahbeelay*]
periodical	periodico [*payreeohdeekoh*]
poem	poesia [*pohayseeah*]
(to) print	stampare [*stahmpahray*]
publishing house	casa editrice [*cahsah aydeetreechay*]
reprint	ristampa [*reestahmpah*]
science fiction book	libro di fantascienza [*leebroh dee fahntahsheeayntsah*]
short story	novella [*nohvelllah*]
subscription	abbonamento [*ahbbohnahmentoh*]
thriller	romanzo giallo [*rohmahntsoh jahlloh*]
volume	volume [*vohloomay*]

Where can I buy English papers?	Dove posso comprare giornali in inglese? [*dohvay posssoh komprahray jorrnahlee een eenglaysay?*]
Where's the guide-book section?	Dov'è il reparto delle guide turistiche? [*dohvay eel raypahrtoh delllay gweeday tooreesteekay?*]
I want a map of the town, showing the monuments	Desidero una pianta della città con segnati i monumenti [*dayzeedayroh oonah peeahntah delllah cheettah kon saynyahtee ee mohnoomenntee*]
I'd like a motoring map of the whole of Italy	Vorrei una carta automobilistica di tutta l'Italia [*vorrayee oonah kahrtah owtohmohbeeleesteekah dee toottah leetahleeah*]
Do you have second-hand books?	Avete libri d'occasione? [*ahvaytay leebree dokkahzeeohnay*]
I'd like an Italian dictionary	Vorrei un dizionario italiano [*vorrayee oon deetseeohnahreeoh eetahleeahnoh*]
Please show me the catalogue of your publications	Per favore mostratemi il catologo delle vostre edizioni [*pehr fahvohray mosstrahtaymee eel kahtahlohgoh delllay vohstray aydeetseeohnee*]
Have you got the latest novel by...?	Ha l'ultimo romanzo di...? [*ah loolteemoh rohmahntsoh dee...?*]

I want to subscribe to this magazine	Voglio abbonarmi a questa rivista [*vohlyoh ahbbohnahrmee a qwesstah reeveestah*]
What is the subscription for a year?	Quant'è l'abbonamento annuale? [*qwahntay lahbbohnahmentoh ahnnooahlay?*]

AT THE BUTCHER'S

beef	manzo [*mahntzoh*]
black-pudding	sanguinaccio [*sahnggweenahchchoh*]
chicken	pollo [*pohllloh*]
chicken breast	petto di pollo [*paytttoh dee pohllloh*]
chop	cotoletta [*kohtohlettah*]
fillet	filetto [*feeletttoh*]
frozen meat	carne congelata [*kahrnay kohnjaylahtah*]
game	selvaggina [*sellvahdjeenah*]
giblets	frattaglie [*frahtttahlyeeay*]
horse meat	carne equina [*kahrnay aykweenah*]
kid	capretto [*kahpraytttoh*]
lamb	agnello [*ahnyellloh*]
liver	fegato [*faygahtoh*]
marrowbone	osso buco [*ohssoh bookoh*]
meat	carne [*kahrnay*]
meat in thin slices	carne a fette sottili [*kahrnay ah fettay sotteelee*]
minced meat	carne tritata [*kahrnay treetahtah*]
mutton	montone [*mohntohnay*]
pork	maiale [*maheeahlay*]
rabbit	coniglio [*kohneelyoh*]
roast meat	arrosto [*ahrrohstoh*]
rump	girello [*jeerellloh*]
sausage	salsiccia [*sahlseechchah*]
sirloin	lombata [*lohmbahtah*]
steak	bistecca [*beestaykkah*]
tripe	trippa [*treeppah*]
turkey	tacchino [*tahkkeenoh*]
veal	vitello [*veetellloh*]
veal steak	fesa [*faysah*]

CHEMIST'S SHOP

see p. 112

CLOTHES

anorak	giacca a vento [*jahkkah ah ventoh*]
bathing cap	cuffia da bagno [*koofyah dah bahnyoh*]
bathing suit	costume da bagno [*kohstoomay dah bahnyoh*]

bathrobe	accappatoio [*ahkkahpahtohyoh*]
belt	cintura [*cheentoorah*]
beret	basco [*bahskoh*]
bib	bavaglino [*bahvahlyeenoh*]
blouse	camicetta [*kahmeechettah*]
blue jeans	blue jeans
bow tie	cravatta a farfalla [*krahvahttah ah fahrfahllah*]
braces	bretelle [*braytelllay*]
brassière	reggiseno [*raydjeesaynoh*]
breast: single breasted; double breasted	petto: a un petto; doppio petto [*pettoh: ah oon pettoh; doppeeoh pettoh*]
cap	berretto [*behrrettoh*]
cardigan	golf, aperto davanti, con bottoni [*golf ahpehrtoh dahvahntee kon bottohnee*]
cloth	stoffa [*stofffah*]
coat	cappotto [*kahppottoh*]
collar	colletto [*kollettoh*]
cotton	cotone [*kohtohnay*]
cut	taglio [*tahlyoh*]
dress	abito per donna [*ahbeetoh pehr donnah*]
dressing gown	vestaglia [*vesstahlyah*]
embroidery	ricamo [*reekahmoh*]
evening dress	abito da sera [*ahbeetoh dah sayrah*]
fashion parade	sfilata di moda [*sfeelahtah dee mohdah*]
fur-coat	pelliccia [*pellleechchah*]
girdle	busto [*boostoh*]
gloves	guanti [*gwahntee*]
half sleeves shirt	camicia a maniche corte [*kahmeechah ah mahneekay kohrtay*]
handbag	borsetta [*borrsayttah*]
handkerchief	fazzoletto [*fahtzohlettoh*]
hat	cappello [*kahppellloh*]
hem	orlo [*orloh*]
jacket	giacca [*jahkkah*]
jumper	pullover di lana [*poollohvehr dee lahnah*]
leather gloves	guanti di pelle [*gwahntee dee pelllay*]
linen	lino [*leenoh*]
lining	fodera [*fohdayrah*]
long sleeves shirt	camicia a maniche lunghe [*kahmeechah ah mahneekay loongay*]
miniskirt	minigonna [*meeneegonnah*]
neckline	scollatura [*skolllahtoorah*]
night dress	camicia da notte [*kahmeechah dah nottay*]
nylon stockings	calze di nylon [*kahltzay dee nylon*]
overalls	tuta [*tootah*]
overcoat	soprabito [*sohprahbeetoh*]
panties	mutande da donna [*mootahnday dah donnah*]

pattern	modello [*mohdellloh*]
pattern tie	cravatta fantasia [*krahvahttah fahntahseeah*]
petticoat	sottoveste [*sottohvesstay*]
plain tie	cravatta in tinta unita [*krahvahttah een teentah ooneetah*]
pleat	piega [*peeaygah*]
pocket	tasca [*tahskah*]
pyjamas	pigiama [*peejahmah*]
raincoat	impermeabile [*eempehrmayahbeelay*]
roll-neck pullover	pullover a collo alto [*pullover ah kollloh ahltoh*]
rompers	tutina per neonati [*tooteenah pehr nayohnahtee*]
scarf	sciarpa [*shahrpah*]
sheepskin	montone [*mohntohnay*]
shirt	camicia [*kahmeechah*]
shorts	calzoncini [*kahltsoncheenee*]
signed dress (suit)	vestito firmato [*vessteetoh feermahtoh*]
silk	seta [*saytah*]
size	taglia [*tahlyah*]
skirt	gonna [*gonnah*]
sleeve	manica [*mahneekah*]
socks	calzini [*kahltzeenee*]
stockings	calze da donna [*kahltzay dah donnah*]
striped tie	cravatta a strisce [*krahvahttah ah streehshay*]
suit	abito per uomo [*ahbeetoh pehr ooohmoh*]
suspenders	reggicalze [*raydjeekahltzay*]
sweater	maglione [*mahlyohnay*]
swimsuit	costume da bagno [*kohstoomay dah bahnyoh*]
T-shirt	maglietta di cotone [*mahlyayttah dee kohtohnay*]
tie	cravatta [*krahvahttah*]
tights	collants
tracksuit	tuta sportiva [*tootah sporrteevah*]
trousers	pantaloni [*pahntahlohnee*]
underpants	slip [*sleep*]
undervest	canottiera [*kahnottteeayrah*]
waistcoat	panciotto [*pahnchottoh*]
wool	lana [*lahnah*]

I'd like a miniskirt	Vorrei una minigonna [*vorrayee oonah meeneegonnah*]
I like the one in the window	Mi piace quella in vetrina [*mee peeahchay kwellah een vaytreenah*]
What's it made of?	Di che cos'è? [*dee kay kosay?*]
Do you have any better quality?	Ha una qualità migliore? [*ha oonah kwaleetah meelyohray?*]

Is it hand washable?	Si può lavare a mano? [*see poooh lahvahray ah mahnoh?*]
Will it shrink?	Si restringerà? [*see resstreenjayrah*]
I take size 44	La mia taglia è il 44 [*lah meeah tahlyah ay eel 44*]
I don't know the Italian sizes	Non conosco le misure italiane [*nonn kohnohskoh lay meezooray eetahleeahnay*]
Can I try it on?	Posso provarla? [*posssoh prohvahrlah?*]
Where is the fitting room?	Dov'è la cabina di prova? [*dohvay lah cahbeenah dee prohvah?*]
It fits very well	Va molto bene [*vah mohltoh baynay*]
It doesn't fit	Non va bene [*nonn vah baynay*]
It's too loose	È troppo larga [*ay troppoh lahrgah*]
I'd like this pair of trousers	Vorrei questo paio di pantaloni [*vohrrayee kwesstoh pahyoh dee pahntahlohnee*]
It seems a wonderful bargain	Pare un ottimo affare [*pahray oon otteemoh ahffahray*]
Could you tell me where I can find wool and silk materials?	Mi può dire dove posso trovare tessuti di lana e di seta? [*mee poooh deeray dohvay possoh trohvahray tesssootee dee lahnah ay dee saytah?*]

FISH-SHOP

anchovy	acciuga [*ahchchoogah*]
cod	merluzzo [*mehrlootzoh*]
crab	gambero [*gahmbayroh*]
cuttle-fish	seppia [*seppeeah*]
eel	anguilla [*ahnggweellah*]
lobster	aragosta [*ahrahgohstah*]
oyster	ostrica [*ohstreekah*]
polyp	polipo [*pohleepoh*]
salmon	salmone [*sahlmohnay*]
sardine	sardina [*sahrdeenah*]
shrimp	gamberetto [*gahmbayrayttoh*]
sole	sogliola [*sohlyohlah*]
squid	calamaro [*kahlahmahroh*]
trout	trota [*trohtah*]
tuna, tunny fish	tonno [*tohnnoh*]
turbot	rombo [*rohmboh*]
whiting	nasello [*nahsaylloh*]

FLORIST

azalea	azalea [*ahtsahlayah*]
cactus	pianta grassa [*peeahntah grahsssah*]
carnation	garofano [*gahrohfahnoh*]
chrysanthemum	crisantemo [*kreezahntaymoh*]
cyclamen	ciclamino [*cheeklahmeenoh*]

daffodil	narciso [*nahrcheesoh*]
dahlia	dalia [*dahleeah*]
daisy	margherita [*mahrgayreetah*]
forget-me-not	myosotis [*meeohsohtees*]
gardenia	gardenia [*gahrdayneeah*]
geranium	geranio [*jayrahneeoh*]
gladiolus	gladiolo [*glahdeeohloh*]
hyacinth	giacinto [*jahcheentoh*]
iris	iris [*eerees*]
lilac	lillà [*leellah*]
lily	giglio [*jeelyoh*]
lily-of-the-valley	mughetto [*mooghettoh*]
mimosa	mimosa [*meemohsah*]
narcissus	narciso [*nahrcheezoh*]
orchid	orchidea [*orrkeedayah*]
pansy	viola del pensiero [*veeohlah dell pehnseeayroh*]
primrose	primula [*preemoolah*]
rose	rosa [*rohzah*]
snow-drop	bucaneve [*bookahnayvay*]
tulip	tulipano [*tooleepahnoh*]
violet	violetta [*veeohlayttah*]
wistaria	glicine [*gleecheenay*]

I want a bunch of wild flowers	Desidero un mazzo di fiori di campagna [*dayseedayroh oon mahtzoh dee feeohree dee kahmpahnyah*]
I want a flower pot	Desidero una pianta in vaso [*dayseedayroh oonah peeahntah een vahsoh*]
Please, send these flowers to this address with my card	Per favore recapiti questi fiori al seguente indirizzo con questo biglietto [*pehr fahvohray raykahpeetee kwesstee feeohree ahl saygwayntay eendeereetzoh kon qwesstoh beelyettoh*]
I'd like to send twelve red roses to Rome through Fleurop	Vorrei mandare dodici rose rosse a Roma tramite Fleurop [*vorrayee mahndahray dohdeechee rohzay rohsssay ah rohmah trahmeetay fleurop*]

AT THE GREENGROCER'S

almond	mandorla [*mahndorrrlah*]
apple	mela [*maylah*]
apricot	albicocca [*ahlbeekockkah*]
artichoke	carciofo [*kahrchohfoh*]
asparagus	asparago [*ahspahrahgoh*]
bean	fagiolo [*fahjohloh*]
beetroot	barbabietola [*bahrbahbeeaytohlah*]
cabbage	cavolo [*kahvohloh*]
carrot	carota [*kahrohtah*]

cauliflower	cavolfiore [*kahvohlfyohray*]
celery	sedano [*saydahnoh*]
cherry	ciliegia [*cheeleeayjah*]
chicory	cicoria [*cheekohreeah*]
cucumber	cetriolo [*chaytreeohloh*]
fig	fico [*feekoh*]
French beans	fagiolini [*fahjohleenee*]
garlic	aglio [*ahlyoh*]
grapes	uva [*oovah*]
lemon	limone [*leemohnay*]
lettuce	lattuga [*lahttoogah*]
mushroom	fungo [*foonggoh*]
onion	cipolla [*cheepolllah*]
orange	arancia [*ahrahnchah*]
parsley	prezzemolo [*pretsaymohloh*]
pea-nut	arachide [*ahrahkeeday*]
peach	pesca [*pesskah*]
pear	pera [*payrah*]
peas	piselli [*peezelllee*]
plum	prugna [*proonyah*]
potato	patata [*pahtahtah*]
pumpkin	zucca [*tsookkah*]
radish	ravanello [*rahvahnellloh*]
salad	insalata [*eensahlahtah*]
spinach	spinaci [*speenahchee*]
strawberry	fragola [*frahgohlah*]
tangerine	mandarino [*mahndahreenoh*]
tomato	pomodoro [*pohmohdohroh*]
turnip	rapa [*rahpah*]
vegetable marrow	zucchina [*tsookkeenah*]
walnut	noce [*nohchay*]

I'd like a kilo of potatoes	Vorrei un chilo di patate [*vorrayee oon keeloh dee pahtahtay*]
Can I have half a kilo of apricots?	Posso avere mezzo chilo di albicocche? [*posssoh ahvayray medzoh keeloh dee ahlbeekockkay*]

1 kilogram or kilo (kg) = 1000 grams (g)

100 g = 3.5 oz.	1/2 kg = 1.1 lbs.
200 g = 7.0 oz.	1 kg = 2.2 lbs.

1 oz. = 28.35 g
1 lb. = 453.60 g

AT THE GROCER'S

bouillon cube	dado per brodo [*dahdoh pehr brohdoh*]
cloves	chiodi di garofano [*keeohdee dee gahrohfahnoh*]

cocoa	cacao [*kahkahoh*]
coffee in beans, ground coffee	caffè in chicchi, caffè macinato [*kahffay een keekkee, kahffay mahcheenahtoh*]
corned beef and other tinned meat	carne in scatola [*kahrnay een skahtohlah*]
dried fruit	frutta secca [*froottah seckkah*]
honey	miele [*meeaylay*]
jam	marmellata [*mahrmelllahtah*]
macaroni	maccheroni [*mahkkayrohnee*]
milk in tins, in tubes	latte condensato in scatola, in tubetto [*lahttay kondensahtoh een skahtohlah, een toobayttoh*]
mustard	senape [*saynahpay*]
nutmeg	noce moscata [*nohchay mohskahtah*]
oat flakes	fiocchi d'avena [*feeockkee dahvaynah*]
olive oil	olio d'oliva [*ohleeoh dohleevah*]
pasta	pasta [*pahstah*]
peanut oil	olio d'arachide [*ohleeoh dahrahkeeday*]
peeled tomatoes	pomodori pelati [*pohmohdohree paylahtee*]
pepper	pepe [*paypay*]
pickles	sottaceti [*sottahchaytee*]
raisins	uva secca [*oovah seckkah*]
rice	riso [*reesoh*]
saffron	zafferano [*dsafffayrahnoh*]
seed-oil	olio di semi [*ohleeoh dee saymee*]
sugar	zucchero [*tsookkayroh*]
sunflower oil	olio di girasole [*ohleeoh dee jeerahsohlay*]
tea in bags, leaves	tè in bustine, sciolto [*tay een boossteenay, shoîltoh*]
vinegar	aceto [*ahchaytoh*]
I'd like a packet of tea	Vorrei un pacchetto di tè [*vorrayee oon pahkkettoh dee tay*]
I want a jar of jam and a tin of peaches	Desidero un vasetto di marmellata e una scatola di pesche [*dayzeedayroh oon vahsayttoh dee mahrmelllahtah ay oonah skahtohlah dee pesskay*]
A tube of mustard, please	Un tubetto di mostarda, per favore [*oon toobayttoh dee mosstahrdah, pehr fahvohray*]
Can I have one of those, please?	Posso avere uno di quelli, per favore? [*posssoh ahvayray oonoh dee kwellee pehr fahvohray?*]

JEWELLER

bracelet	braccialetto [*brahchchahlettoh*]
branched candlestick	candelabro [*kahndaylahbroh*]
brooch	spilla [*speellah*]

cake-slice	paletta da dolci [*pahlettah dah dohlchee*]
cameo	cammeo [*kahmmayoh*]
carat	carato [*kahrahtoh*]
chain	catena [*kahtaynah*]
coffee set	servizio da caffè [*sehrveetseeoh dah kahffay*]
coral	corallo [*khorahllloh*]
cuff links	gemelli da polsini [*jaymelllee dah pohlseenee*]
cultured pearl	perla coltivata [*pehrlah kohlteevahtah*]
diamond	diamante [*deeahmahntay*]
ear-rings	orecchini [*ohreckkeenee*]
emerald	smeraldo [*smayrahldoh*]
gold	oro [*ohroh*]
incision	incisione [*eencheeseeohnay*]
medallion	medaglione [*maydahlyeeohnay*]
necklace	collana [*kohlllahnah*]
pearl	perla [*pehrlah*]
platinum	platino [*plahteenoh*]
precious stone	pietra preziosa [*peeaytrah praytseeohsah*]
pewter	peltro [*pehltroh*]
ring	anello [*ahnellloh*]
ruby	rubino [*roobeenoh*]
sapphire	zaffiro [*dsahffeeroh*]
(to) set	montare [*montahray*]
setting	montatura [*montahtoorah*]
silver, silver-plated	argento, argentato [*ahrjentoh, ahrjentahtoh*]
topaz	topazio [*tohpahtseeoh*]
wedding ring	fede [*fayday*]
I want to see some gold chains	Desidero vedere delle catene d'oro [*dayzeedayroh vaydayray delllay kahtaynay dohroh*]
Can you rethread this necklace?	Potete infilare questa collana? [*pohtaytay eeenfeelahray kwesstah kohllahnah?*]
When will it be ready?	Quando sarà pronta? [*kwahndoh sahrah prohntah?*]
How many carats is this diamond?	Di quanti carati è questo brillante? [*dee kwantee kahrahtee ay kwesstoh breellahntay?*]

LAUNDRY/DRY-CLEANER'S

automatic laundry	lavanderia automatica [*lahvahndayreeah owtohmahteekah*]
(to) clean	smacchiare [*smahkkeeahray*]
(to) dry-clean	lavare a secco [*lahvahray ah seckkoh*]
(to) dye	tingere [*teenjayray*]

faded	sbiadito [*sbeeahdeetoh*]
(to) iron	stirare [*steerahray*]
(to) mend	rammendare [*rahmmayndahray*]
(to) patch	rattoppare [*rahttohppahray*]
(to) press	stirare a vapore [*steerahray ah vahpohray*]
(to) remove stains	togliere le macchie [*tollyayray lay mahkkeeay*]
(to) stitch	cucire [*coocheeray*]
(to) wash	lavare [*lahvahray*]

I want these clothes cleaned for tomorrow	Desidero questi abiti puliti per domani [*dayzeedayroh kwesstee ahbeetee pooleetee pehr dohmahnee*]
Can you remove this stain?	Può togliere questa macchia? [*poooh tollyayray kwesstah mahkkeeah?*]
Can this be invisibly mended?	Mi può fare un rammendo invisibile? [*mee poooh fahray oon rahmmayndoh eenveeseebeelay?*]
Is my laundry ready?	È pronta la mia biancheria? [*ay prohntah lah meeah beeahngkayreeah?*]
There is something missing	Manca qualcosa [*mahnkah kwahlkohsah*]
When will my clothes be ready?	Quando saranno pronti i miei abiti? [*kwahndoh sahrahnnoh prohntee ee meeayee ahbeetee?*]

OPTICIAN

astigmatic	astigmatico [*ahsteegmahteekoh*]
binoculars	binocolo [*beenohkohloh*]
contact lenses	lenti a contatto [*layntee ah kohntahtttoh*]
contact lenses fluid	liquido per lenti a contatto [*leekweedoh pehr layntee ah kohntahttoh*]
dioptres	diottrie [*deeohtttreeay*]
frame	montatura [*mohntahtoorah*]
glasses	occhiali [*ockkeeahlee*]
magnifying lens	lente da ingrandimento [*layntay dah eengrahndeementoh*]
opera glasses	binocolo da teatro [*beenohkohloh dah tayahtroh*]
(to) see	vedere [*vaydayray*]
sight	vista [*veestah*]
short sighted/long sighted	miope/presbite [*meeohpay/pressbeetay*]
spectacles	occhiali [*ockkeeahlee*]
spectacle case	astuccio per occhiali [*ahstoochchoh pehr ockkeeahlee*]
spectacle lens	lente da occhiali [*layntay dah ockkeeahlee*]

squint	strabismo [*strabeezmoh*]
sun glasses	occhiali da sole [*ockkeeahlee dah sohlay*]
visual defects	difetti della vista [*deefayttee delllah veestah*]

I'd like to have my eyesight checked	Vorrei farmi controllare la vista [*vorrayee fahrmee kontrolllahray lah veestah*]
I can only read the first three lines of the chart	Leggo soltanto le prime tre righe del cartellone [*layggoh sohltahntoh lay preemay tray reeghay dell kahrtelllohnay*]
I'm short-sighted	Sono miope [*sohnoh meeohpay*]
I've broken my glasses	Ho rotto gli occhiali [*oh rohttoh lyee ockkeeahlee*]
When will they be ready?	Quando saranno pronti? [*kwahndoh sahrahnnoh prohntee?*]
Can you change the lenses?	Può cambiare le lenti? [*poooh kahmbeeayray lay layntee?*]
I've lost one of my contact lenses	Ho perso una lente a contatto [*oh pehrsoh oonah layntay ah kohntahttoh*]
I have hard/soft lenses	Uso lenti a contatto rigide/morbide [*oozoh layntee ah kohntahttoh reejeeday/morrbeeday*]
I want some contact-lens fluid	Desidero del liquido per lenti a contatto [*dayzeedayroh dell leekweedoh pehr layntee ah kohntahttoh*]

PERFUMERY

after-shave lotion	lozione dopobarba [*lohtseeohnay dohpohbahrbah*]
cream	crema [*kraymah*]
deodorant	deodorante [*dayohdohrahntay*]
emery board	limetta per unghie [*leemayttah pehr oonggheeay*]
eye pencil	matita per occhi [*mahteetah pehr ockkee*]
hair lotion	lozione per capelli [*lotseeohnay pehr kahpelllee*]
lipsalve	burro di cacao [*boorroh dee kahkahoh*]
lipstick	rossetto [*rosssayttoh*]
nail file	lima da unghie [*leemah dah oonggheeay*]
nail polish	smalto [*smahltoh*]
nail polish remover	solvente [*sohlvayntay*]
perfume	profumo [*prohfoomoh*]
powder	cipria [*cheepreeah*]
razor blades	lamette [*lahmayttay*]
shaving cream	crema da barba [*kraymah dah bahrbah*]
soap	saponetta [*sahpohnayttah*]

sun-tan cream	crema solare [*kraymah sohlahray*]
talcum powder	talco [*tahlkoh*]
toothbrush	spazzolino da denti [*spahtsohleenoh dah dayntee*]
toothpaste	dentifricio [*daynteefreechoh*]
tweezers	pinzette [*peentsayttay*]

PHOTOGRAPHY

camera	macchina fotografica [*mahkkkeenah fohtohgrahfeekah*]
case	custodia [*koostohdeeah*]
cine camera	cinepresa [*cheenaypraysah*]
colour photo	fotografia a colori [*fohtohgrahfeeah ah kohlohree*]
dark room	camera oscura [*kahmayrah osskoorah*]
(to) develop	sviluppare [*sveelooppahray*]
development	sviluppo [*sveelooppoh*]
(to) enlarge	ingrandire [*eengrahndeeray*]
enlargement	ingrandimento [*eengrahndeementoh*]
(to) expose	esporre [*essporrray*]
exposure (to light)	esposizione [*ayspohseetseeohnay*]
exposure meter	esposimetro [*ayspohseemaytroh*]
exposure time	(tempo) di posa [*tehmpoh dee pohsah*]
film	pellicola [*pellleekohlah*]
filter	filtro [*feeltroh*]
(to) focus	mettere a fuoco [*mettayray ah fooohkoh*]
glossy paper	carta lucida [*kahrtah loocheedah*]
lens	obiettivo [*obyetteevoh*]
light	luce [*loochay*]
(to) load the camera	caricare la macchina [*kahreekahray lah mahkkeenah*]
mat paper	carta opaca [*kahrtah ohpahkah*]
negative	negativa [*naygahteevah*]
out of focus	sfocato [*sfohkahtoh*]
passport size	formato tessera [*fohrmahtoh tesssayrah*]
(to) photograph	fotografare [*fohtohgrahfahray*]
photograph	fotografia [*fohtohgrahfeeah*]
plate	lastra [*lahstrah*]
polarizing filter	filtro polarizzatore [*feeltroh pohlahreetstsahtohray*]
positive	positiva [*pohzeeteevah*]
print	stampa [*stahmpah*]
projector	proiettore [*prohyettohray*]
range-finder camera	macchina fotografica a telemetro [*mahkkeenah fohtohgrahfeekah ah taylaymaytroh*]
release	scatto [*skahttoh*]
roll of film	rotolo di pellicola [*rohtohloh dee pellleekohlah*]

shutter	otturatore [*ohttoorahtohray*]
slide	diapositiva [*deeahpohzeeteevah*]
snap-shot	istantanea [*eestahntahnayah*]
(to) take a blank	scattare a vuoto [*skahttahray ah vooohtoh*]
telephoto lens	teleobiettivo [*taylayohbeeayttteevoh*]
transparency	visore per diapositive [*veesohray pehr deeahpohzeeteevay*]
view finder	mirino [*meereenoh*]

I'd like to have some passport photos taken	Vorrei che mi facesse delle foto per il passaporto [*vorrayee kay mee fahchessay dellay fohtoh pehr eel pahssahporrtoh*]
I'd like a 24 exposure	Vorrei un rullino da 24 [*vorrayee oon roollleenoh dah vehnteekwahttroh*]
Could you load it, please?	Me lo carica per favore? [*may loh kahreekah pehr fahvohray*?]
How much do you charge for developing?	Quanto fate pagare lo sviluppo? [*kwahntoh fahtay pahgahray loh sveelooppoh*?]
Print only the good copies please	Stampi solo le copie riuscite [*stahmpee sohloh lay kohpeeay reeoosheetay*]
I want a black and white film for this camera	Desidero una pellicola in bianco e nero per questa macchina [*dayzeedayroh oonah pellleekohlah een beeahngkoh ay nayroh pehr kwesstah mahkkkeenah*]
There's something wrong with the flash attachment	Non funziona l'attaccatura del flash [*nonn foontseeohnah lahttahkkahtoorah dell flash*]
The film is jammed	La pellicola è bloccata [*lah pellleekohlah ay blockkahtah*]
Can you repair this camera?	Può riparare questa macchina? [*poooh reepahrahray kwesstah mahkkkeenah*?]
When will the photos be ready?	Quando saranno pronte le foto? [*kwahndoh sahrahnnoh prohntay lay fohtoh*?]

SHOE-SHOP

Shoes-Men

American British	5	6	7	8	8 1/2	9	9 1/2	10	11
Continental	38	39	41	42	43	43	44	44	45

Shoes-Women

American British	5	5 1/2	6	6 1/2	7	7 1/2	8
Continental	36	37	38	39	40	41	42

boots — stivali [*steevahlee*]
calf shoes — scarpe di vitello [*skahrpay dee veetellloh*]
climbing boots — scarponi da montagna [*skahrpohnee dah montahnyah*]
clogs — zoccoli [*tsockkohlee*]
foot — piede [*peeayday*]
fur-lined — foderato di pelo [*fohdayrahtoh dee payloh*]
gym shoes — scarpe da ginnastica [*skahrpay dah jeennahsteekah*]
heel — tacco [*tahkkoh*]
high heel — tacco alto [*tahkkoh ahltoh*]
kid shoes — scarpe di capretto [*skahrpay dee kahprehttoh*]
lace — stringa [*streengah*]
leather shoes — scarpe di cuoio [*skahrpay dee kooohyoh*]
low heel — tacco basso [*tahkkoh bahssoh*]
mocassin — mocassino [*mohkassseenoh*]
(to) nail — inchiodare [*eenkeeohdahray*]
orthopedic shoes — scarpe ortopediche [*skahrpay orrtohpaydeekay*]
patent leather — vernice [*vehrneechay*]
plimsolls — scarpe da tennis [*skahrpay dah tennis*]
(to) polish — lucidare [*loocheedahray*]
(to) put on the last — mettere in forma [*mettayray een fohrmah*]
quick repairs — riparazione rapida [*reepahrahtseeohnay rahpeedah*]
(to) re-sole — risuolare [*reesooohlahray*]
rubber sole — suola di para [*sooholah dee pahrah*]
sandal — sandalo [*sahndahloh*]
shoe — scarpa [*skahrpah*]
shoe-brush — spazzola da scarpe [*spahtsohlah dah skahrpay*]
shoe-horn — corno per calzature [*korrnoh pehr kahltzahtooray*]

shoe polish	lucido da scarpe [*loocheedoh dah skahrpay*]
size	misura [*meezoorah*]
slipper	pantofola [*pahntohfohlah*]
(to) stick	incollare [*eenkollahray*]
suede	scamosciato [*skahmohshahtoh*]
toe (of shoe)	punta [*poontah*]
(to) try on shoes	provare le scarpe [*prohvahray lay skahrpay*]

Can I see those flat shoes in the window?	Posso vedere quelle scarpe basse in vetrina? [*posssoh vaydayray kwelllay skahrpay bahssay een vaytreenah*]
I take size 6	Porto il numero 38 [*pohrtoh eel noomayroh trayntohttoh*]
Unfortunately, these are too narrow	Purtroppo sono strette [*poortroppoh sohno strayttay*]
Can I try a pair half a size larger?	Posso provare un mezzo numero più grande? [*posssoh prohvahray oon medzoh noomayroh peeoo grahnday*?]
Do you have the same in black?	Ha le stesse in nero? [*ah lay stesssay een nayroh*?]
These are all right, I'll take them	Queste vanno bene, le prendo [*kwesstay vahnnoh baynay lay prendoh*]
How much are they?	Quanto? [*kwahntoh*?]
I need some shoelaces	Mi servono dei lacci [*mee sehrvohnoh dayee lahchchee*]
These shoes have come unsewm, can you repair them?	Queste scarpe sono scucite, le può riparare? [*kwesstay skahrpay sohnoh skoocheetay, lay poooh reepahrahray*]
I need them as soon as possible	Mi servono al più presto possibile [*mee sehrvohnoh ahl peeoo presstoh possseebeelay*]
I want new soles and heels	Desidero suole e tacchi nuovi [*dayzeedayroh sooohlay ay tahkkee nooohvee*]
This heel has come off, can you stick it?	Questo tacco si è staccato, lo può incollare? [*kwesstoh tahkkoh see ay stahkkahtoh, loh poooh eenkolllahray*?]

STATIONERY

address book	rubrica [*roobreekah*]
ball-point pen	biro [*beeroh*]
card	cartoncino [*kahrtohncheenoh*]
calendar	calendario [*kahlayndahreeoh*]
carbon paper	carta carbone [*kahrtah kahrbohnay*]
cellophane tape	nastro adesivo [*nahstroh ahdayzeevoh*]
drawing paper	carta da disegno [*kahrtah dah deesaynyoh*]
drawing pins	puntine [*poonteenay*]

envelope	busta [*boostah*]
eraser	gomma [*gohmmah*]
exercise-book	quaderno [*kwahdehrnoh*]
felt-tip pen	pennarello [*pennahraylllloh*]
fountain pen	penna stilografica [*pennah steelohgrahfeekah*]
glue	colla [*kolllah*]
adhesive labels	etichette adesive [*ayteekettay ahdayzeevay*]
notebook	taccuino [*takkooeenoh*]
note paper	carta da lettere [*kahrtah dah lettayray*]
paintbox	scatola di colori [*skahtohlah dee kohlohree*]
paperback	libro tascabile [*leebroh tahskahbeelay*]
paperclips	fermagli [*fehrmahlyee*]
pen	penna [*pennnah*]
pencil	matita [*mahteetah*]
pencil sharpener	temperamatite [*tempayrahmahteetay*]
playing cards	carte da gioco [*kahrtay dah jooohkoh*]
pocket calculator	calcolatore tascabile [*kahlkohlahtohray tahskahbeelay*]
postcard	cartolina [*kahrtohleenah*]
refill (for a pen)	ricambio [*reekahmbeeoh*]
rubber	gomma [*gohmmah*]
staples	graffette [*grahffettay*]
tissue paper	carta velina [*kahrtah vayleenah*]
typewriter ribbon	nastro per macchina da scrivere [*nahstroh pehr mahkkkeenah dah skreevayray*]
typing paper	carta per macchina da scrivere [*kahrtah pehr mahkkkeenah dah skreevayray*]
writing pad	blocco per appunti [*blockkoh pehr ahppoontee*]

I want some picture postcards with views of the town	Desidero cartoline illustrate con vedute della città [*dayzeedayroh kahrtohleenay eelloostrahtay kon vaydootay delllah cheettah*]
Can I have a squared exercise?	Posso avere un quaderno a quadretti? [*posssoh ahvayray oon kwahdehrnoh ah kwahdrayttee*]
I'd like a soft black pencil	Vorrei una matita nera molle [*vorrayee oonah mahteetah nayrah molllay*]
Have you any sheets of wrapping paper and a ball of string?	Avete dei fogli di carta da pacchi e un gomitolo di spago? [*ahvaytay dayee follyee dee kahrtah dah pahkkee ay oon gohmeetohloh dee spahgoh*]

TOBACCONIST'S

> You can recognize a tobacconist's by a large white 'T' on a black background. You can buy stamps at the tobacconist's.

a carton	una stecca [*oonah staykkah*]
candy	caramella [*kahramaylllah*]
cigar	sigaro [*seegahroh*]
cigarette	sigaretta [*seegahrettah*]
cigarette case	portasigarette [*porrtahseegahrettay*]
cigarette holder	bocchino [*bockkeenoh*]
cigar-lighter	accendisigari [*ahchchendeeseegahree*]
cigarette-papers	cartine per sigarette [*kahrteenay pehr seegahrettay*]
cigarette-tobacco	tabacco da sigarette [*tahbahkkoh dah seegahrettay*]
cigarette with/without filter	sigarette con o senza filtro [*seegahrettay kon/sentsah feeltroh*]
havana cigar	sigaro avana [*seegahroh ahvahnah*]
hookah	pipa turca [*peepah toorkah*]
king-size cigarette	sigarette formato lungo [*seegahrettay fohrmahtoh loongoh*]
lighter	accendino [*ahchchayndeenoh*]
lighter fluid/gas	benzina/gas per accendino [*bendzeenah/gahs pehr ahchchayndeenoh*]
matches	fiammiferi [*feeahmmeefayree*]
pipe	pipa [*peepah*]
pipe cleaner	nettapipe [*nettahpeepay*]
reserve flints	pietrine di riserva [*peeaytreenay dee reesehrvah*]
safety matches	fiammiferi svedesi [*feeahmmeefayree svaydaysee*]
salt	sale [*sahlay*]
stamps	francobolli [*frahngkohbolllee*]
sweets	caramelle [*kahrahmaylllay*]
tobacco-pouch	tabacchiera [*tahbahkkeeayrah*]

Can I have a packet of cigarettes?	Posso avere un pacchetto di sigarette? [*posssoh ahvayray oon pahkkettoh dee seegahrettay*?]
Can you fill my lighter?	Mi carica l'accendino? [*mee kahreekah lahchchayndeenoh*?]
I'd like some strong cigarettes, filter tips	Vorrei delle sigarette forti con filtro [*vorrayee dellay seegahretttay fohrtee kon feeltroh*]
A stamp for this letter, please	Un francobollo per questa lettera, per favore [*oon frahngkohbollloh pehr kwesstah lettayrah, pehr fahvohray*]

WATCHMAKER

alarm-clock	sveglia [*svaylyah*]
balance staff	asse del bilanciere [*ahssay dell beelahncheeayray*]
case	cassa [*kahssah*]
chronometre	cronometro [*krohnohmaytroh*]
clock	orologio [*ohrohlohjoh*]
dial	quadrante [*kwahdrahntay*]
digital watch	orologio digitale [*ohrohlohjoh deejeetahlay*]
gear	ingranaggio [*eengrahnahdjoh*]
hair-spring	molla [*molllah*]
hand	lancetta [*lahnchettah*]
pocket-watch	orologio da tasca [*ohrohlohjoh dah tahskah*]
quartz watch	orologio al quarzo [*ohrohlohjoh ahl kwahrtsoh*]
(to) repair	riparare [*reepahrahray*]
self-winding watch	orologio automatico [*ohrohlohjoh owtohmahteekoh*]
watch	orologio [*ohrohlohjoh*]
watchstrap	cinturino [*cheentooreenoh*]
(to) wind up	caricare [*kahreekahray*]
wrist-watch	orologio da polso [*ohrohlohjoh dah pohlsoh*]

Can you repair this watch?	Può riparare questo orologio? [*poooh reepahrahray kwesstoh ohrohlohjoh*?]
My watch gains/loses	Il mio orologio è avanti/indietro [*eel meeoh ohrohlohjoh ay ahvahntee/eendeeaytroh*]
Can you change the glass of my watch?	Può cambiare il vetro dell'orologio? [*poooh kahmbeeahray eel vaytroh dellohrohlohjoh*?]
Would you please clean the works?	Per favore mi pulite il meccanismo? [*pehr fahvohray mee pooleetay eel meckkaneesmoh*?]
When will it be ready?	Quando sarà pronto? [*kwahndoh sahrah prohntoh*?]

Xi HEALTH AND MEDICAL ASSISTANCE

PHYSIOLOGY AND PATHOLOGY

Medical advice and treatment are available to British and Irish visitors on the same basis as for Italian subjects. In order to make sure you are treated free of charge, you should take with you form E 111, issued by the Department of Social Security.

PARTS OF THE BODY

ankle	caviglia [*kahveelyah*]
arm	braccio [*brahchchoh*]
artery	arteria [*ahrtayreeah*]
back	schiena [*skeeaynah*]
bladder	vescica [*vaysheekah*]
blood	sangue [*sahnggway*]
body	corpo [*kohrpoh*]
bone	osso [*osssoh*]
breast	seno [*saynoh*]
brain	cervello [*chehrvellloh*]
cheek	guancia [*gwahnchah*]
chest	torace [*tohrahchay*]
chin	mento [*mentoh*]
ear	orecchio [*ohreckkeeoh*]
elbow	gomito [*gohmeetoh*]
eye	occhio [*ockkeeoh*]
face	viso [*veezoh*]
fingers	dita della mano [*deetah delllah mahnoh*]
foot	piede [*peeayday*]
forehead	fronte [*frontay*]
gland	ghiandola [*gheeahndohlah*]
gum	gengiva [*jaynjeevah*]
hair	capelli [*kahpaylllee*]
hand	mano [*mahnoh*]
heart	cuore [*kwohray*]
heel	tallone [*tahllohnay*]
hips	fianchi [*feeahngkee*]
intestine	intestino [*eentessteenoh*]
jaw	mascella [*mahshelllah*]
kidney	rene [*raynay*]
knee	ginocchio [*jeenockkeeoh*]
leg	gamba [*gahmbah*]
lip	labbro [*lahbbroh*]
liver	fegato [*faygahtoh*]
lungs	polmoni [*pollmohnee*]

mouth	bocca [*bockkah*]
muscle	muscolo [*mooskohloh*]
nail	unghia [*oonggheeah*]
neck	collo [*kollloh*]
nerve	nervo [*nehrvoh*]
nervous system	sistema nervoso [*seestaymah nehrvohsoh*]
nose	naso [*nahsoh*]
nostril	narice [*nahreechay*]
palate	palato [*pahlahtoh*]
pelvis	bacino [*bahcheenoh*]
rib	costola [*kohstohlah*]
shoulder	spalla [*spahllah*]
skin	pelle [*pelllay*]
skull	cranio [*krahneeoh*]
spine	spina dorsale [*speenah dorrsahlay*]
stomach	stomaco [*stohmahkoh*]
thigh	coscia [*kohshah*]
thigh bone	femore [*faymohray*]
throat	gola [*gohlah*]
toes	dita del piede [*deetah dell peeayday*]
tongue	lingua [*leenggwah*]
tonsils	tonsille [*tonseelllay*]
thumb	dito pollice [*deetoh pollleechay*]
vein	vena [*vaynah*]
wrist	polso [*pollsoh*]

THE SENSES

hearing-(to) hear	udito-udire (*oodeetoh-oodeeray*]
sight-(to) see	vista-vedere [*veestah-vaydayray*]
smell-(to) smell	odorato-odorare [*ohdohrahtoh-ohdohrahray*]
taste-(to) taste	gusto-gustare [*goostoh-goostahray*]
touch-(to) touch	tatto-tastare [*tahttoh-tahstahray*]

ILLNESSES

Aids	Aids [*aids*]
abstinence crisis	crisi di astinenza [*kreezee dee ahsteenentzah*]
allergy	allergia [*ahllehrjeeah*]
appendicitis	appendicite [*ahppendeecheetay*]
arthritis	artrite [*ahrtreetay*]
asthma	asma [*ahsmah*]
bronchitis	bronchite [*brongkeetay*]
cancer	cancro [*kahngkroh*]
chicken box	varicella [*vahreechelllah*]
colitis	colite [*kohleetay*]
collapse	collasso [*kohlllasssoh*]

concussion of the brain	commozione cerebrale [*kommohtseeohnay chayraybrahlay*]
congestion	congestione [*konjaysteeohnay*]
conjunctivitis	congiuntivite [*konjoonteeveetay*]
convulsive cough	tosse convulsa [*tosssay konvoolsah*]
cystitis	cistite [*cheesteetay*]
deafness	sordità [*sorrdeetah*]
death	morte [*mohrtay*]
diabetis	diabete [*deeahbaytay*]
dislocation	lussazione [*loossahtseeohnay*]
drug addiction	tossicodipendenza [*tohssseekoh-deepayndayntzah*]
epilepsy	epilessia [*aypeelessseeah*]
fainting	svenimento [*svayneemantoh*]
fever	febbre [*febbray*]
flu	influenza [*eenflooayntzah*]
fracture	frattura [*frahttoorah*]
gangrene	cancrena [*kahnkraynah*]
hay fever	febbre da fieno [*febbray dah feeaynoh*]
haemorrage	emorragia [*aymohrrahjeeah*]
heart attack	infarto [*eenfahrtoh*]
hernia	ernia [*ehrneeah*]
indigestion	indigestione [*eendeejessteeohnay*]
infection	infezione [*eenfaytsseohnay*]
influenza	influenza [*eenflooayntzah*]
jaundice	itterizia [*eettayreetzeeah*]
lumbago	lombaggine [*lombahdjeenay*]
measles	morbillo [*morrbeelloh*]
nausea	nausea [*nawzayah*]
nervous breakdown	esaurimento nervoso [*ayzowreementoh nehrvohsoh*]
neuralgia	nevralgia [*nayvrahljeeah*]
otitis	otite [*ohteetay*]
paralysis	paralisi [*pahrahleezee*]
peritonitis	peritonite [*payreetohneetay*]
pneumonia	polmonite [*pohlmohneetay*]
rheumatism	reumatismo [*rayoomahteesmoh*]
scarlet fever	scarlattina [*skahrlahtteenah*]
smallpox	vaiolo [*vaheeohloh*]
sunstroke	colpo di sole [*kollpoh dee sohlay*]
tetanus	tetano [*taytahnoh*]
thrombosis	trombosi [*trombohsee*]
typhus	tifo [*teefoh*]
ulcer	ulcera [*oolchayrah*]
varicose veins	vene varicose [*vaynay vahreekohsay*]
vertigo	vertigini [*vehrteejeenee*]
vomiting	vomito [*vohmeetoh*]

SYMPTOMS

constipation	stitichezza [*steetteeketzah*]
cough	tosse [*tosssay*]
cramp	crampo [*krahmpoh*]
eruption	eruzione [*ayrootseeohnay*]
fainting	svenimento [*svayneementoh*]
fever	febbre [*febbray*]
giddiness	capogiri [*kahpohjeeree*]
head-ache	mal di testa [*mahl dee taystah*]
indisposition	malessere [*mahlesssayray*]
inflammation	infiammazione [*eenfeeahmmahtseeohnay*]
insomnia	insonnia [*eensonneeah*]
nausea	nausea [*nowzayah*]
pains	dolori [*dohlohree*]
palpitations	palpitazioni [*pahlpeetahtseeohnee*]
rash	eruzione [*ayrootseeonay*]
shivers	brividi [*breeveedee*]
sneeze	starnuto [*stahrnootoh*]
sore throat	mal di gola [*mahl dee gohlah*]
stomach ache	mal di pancia [*mahl dee pahnchah*]
stomach burn	bruciore di stomaco [*broochohray dee stomahkoh*]
swelling	gonfiore [*gonfeeohray*]
vomit	vomito [*vohmeetoh*]
weaknesss	spossatezza [*sposssahtetsah*]

MEDICAL ASSISTANCE

TREATMENT

What treatment are you having?	Che cura fa? [*kay kooray fah*?]
I'm receiving treatment for cancer	Mi sto sottoponendo a una cura contro il cancro [*mee stoh sottohpohnayndoh ah oonah koorah kontroh eel kahnkroh*]
I'm allergic to antibiotics	Sono allergico agli antibiotici [*sohnoh ahllayrjeekoh ahlyee ahnteebeeohteechee*]
What can you prescribe for the pain in my back, doctor?	Cosa mi può prescrivere per il mal di schiena? [*kohsah mee poooh presskreevayray pehr eel mahl dee skeeaynah*]
Can you give me a prescription for a tranquillizer?	Può farmi una ricetta per un tranquillante? [*poooh fahrmee oonah reechettah pehr oon trahnkweellahntay*]
How many times a day should I take these pills?	Quante volte al giorno devo prendere queste pillole? [*kwahntay volltay ahl jorrnoh dayvoh prendayray kwesstay peellohhlay*]
Shall I take this medicine before or after each meal?	Devo prendere questa medicina prima o dopo i pasti? [*dayvoh prendayray kwesstah maydeecheenah preemah oh dohpoh ee pahstee*?]
I am pregnant. Can I take a painkiller?	Sono incinta. Posso prendere un calmante? [*sohnoh eencheentah. posssoh prendayray oon kahlmahntay*?]
I am on the pill	Prendo la pillola [*prendoh lah peellohlah*]
Do you want a specimen of my blood?	Vuole un campione del mio sangue? [*vooohlay oon kahmpeeohnay dell meeoh sahnggway*?]

AT THE DOCTOR'S

Is there a doctor here?	C'è un medico qui? [*chay oon maydeekoh kwee*?]
Where's the surgery?	Dov'è l'ambulatorio? [*dohvay lahmboolahtohreeoh*]
What are the surgery hours?	Quali sono le ore di consultazione? [*kwahlee sohnoh lay ohray dee konsooltahtzeeohnay*?]
My ankle is swollen	La mia caviglia è gonfia [*lah meeah kahveelyah ay gonfeeah*]
I can't move my arm	Non posso muovere il braccio [*nonn possoh mooohvayray eel brahchchoh*]

It hurts	Mi fa male [*mee fah mahlay*]
I'm not feeling well	Non mi sento bene [*nonn mee sayntoh baynay*]
I've got a fever	Ho la febbre [*oh lah febbray*]
My blood pressure is too low	La mia pressione è troppo bassa [*lah meeah pressseeohnay ay troppoh bahssah*]
I want to go to the hospital for a general check-up	Voglio andare all'ospedale per un controllo generale [*vollyoh ahndahray ahllosspaydahlay pehr oon kontrollloh jaynayrahlay*]
May I have a receipt for my health insurance?	Posso avere una ricevuta per la mia assicurazione malattia? [*posssoh ahvayray oonah reechayvootah pehr lah meeah ahsseekoorahtseeonay mahlahtteeah?*]
Can I have a medical certificate?	Posso avere un certificato medico? [*posssoh ahvayray oon chehrteefeekahtoh maydeekoh?*]
How much do I owe you?	Quanto devo? [*kwahntoh dayvoh?*]

AT THE DENTIST'S

abscess (on the tooth)	ascesso [*ahshesssoh*]
anaesthetic	anestetico [*ahnesstayteekoh*]
canine tooth	dente canino [*dentay kahneenoh*]
caries	carie [*kahreeay*]
crown	capsula [*kahpsoolah*]
decayed tooth	dente cariato [*dentay kahreeahtoh*]
dental drill	trapano [*trahpahnoh*]
dental plate	dentiera [*denteeayrah*]
dental prothesis	protesi [*prohtaysee*]
denture	dentiera [*denteeayrah*]
disinfection	disinfezione [*deezeenfaytseeohnay*]
enamel	smalto [*smahltoh*]
(to) extract a tooth	estrarre un dente [*esstrahrray oon dentay*]
false tooth	dente falso [*dentay fahlsoh*]
(to) fill	otturare [*ottoorahray*]
filling	otturazione [*ottoorahtseeohnay*]
(to) gargle	fare gargarismi [*fahray gahrgahreezmee*]
gengivitis	gengivite [*jenjeeveetay*]
gum	gengiva [*jenjeevah*]
(to) medicate	medicare [*maydeekahray*]
medication	medicazione [*maydeekahtseeohnay*]
milk tooth	dente di latte [*dentay dee lahttay*]
molar tooth	molare [*mohlahray*]
mouth	bocca [*bockkah*]
nerve	nervo [*nehrvoh*]
(to) pull out	estrarre [*esstrahrray*]

root	radice [*rahdeechay*]
set of teeth	dentatura [*dentahtoorah*]
tartar	tartaro [*tahrtahroh*]
teeth-print	impronta [*eemprohntah*]
tooth	dente [*dentay*]
tooth-ache	mal di denti [*mahl dee dentee*]
tooth-brush	spazzolino [*spahtsohleenoh*]
tooth-paste	dentifricio [*denteefreechoh*]
wisdom tooth	dente del giudizio [*dentay dell joodeetseeoh*]

Can I have an appointment as soon as possible?	Può fissarmi un appuntamento il più presto possibile? [*poooh feessahrmee oon ahppoontahmentoh eel peeoo presstoh possseebeelay*?]
I have a toothache	Ho mal di denti [*oh mahl dee dentee*]
This molar hurts at the bottom	Questo molare mi duole in basso [*kwesstoh mohlahray mee dooohlay een bahssoh*]
I want to see the dentist to have a tooth out	Voglio vedere il dentista per togliermi un dente [*vollyoh vaydayray eel denteestah pehr tollyayrmee oon dentay*]
Could you give me an anaesthetic?	Può farmi l'anestesia? [*poooh fahrmee lahnesstayseeah*?]
I have a decayed tooth. Can you fix it temporarily?	Ho un dente cariato. Può curarlo provvisoriamente? [*oh oon dentay kahreeahtoh. poooh koorahrloh provveezohreeahmentay*?]
Give me a temporary filling	Fatemi un'otturazione provvisoria [*fahtaymee oon ottoorahtseeohnay provveezohreeah*]
I've broken this dental plate	Ho rotto questa dentiera [*oh rottoh kwesstah denteeayrah*]
Can you repair it right now?	La può riparare subito? [*lah poooh reepahrahray soobeetoh*?]
Rinse your mouth, gargle a little	Si sciacqui, faccia un po' di gargarismi [*see shahkkwee; fachchah oon poh dee gahrgahreezmee*]

HOSPITAL

abstinence crisis	crisi di astinenza [*kreesee dee ahsteenayntsah*]
ambulance	ambulanza [*ahmboolahntzah*]
anaesthesia	anestesia [*ahnesstayzeeah*]
antitetanic injection	iniezione antitetanica [*eenyaytseeohnay ahnteetaytahneekah*]
attendant physician	medico curante [*maydeekoh koorahntay*]
bandage	benda, fascia [*bendah, fahshah*]
bedpan	padella [*pahdelllah*]
clinic	clinica [*kleeneekah*]

consultation	consulto [*konsooltoh*]
contagion	contagio [*kontahjoh*]
convalescence	convalescenza [*konvahlayshentzah*]
crisis	crisi [*kreesee*]
delivery	parto [*pahrtoh*]
diagnosis	diagnosi [*deeahnyohzee*]
disinfection	disinfezione [*deezeenfaytseeohnay*]
epidemic	epidemia [*aypeedaymeeah*]
fit	attacco [*ahttahkkoh*]
head physician	primario [*preemahreeoh*]
hypodermoclysis	ipodermoclisi [*eepohdayrmohkleesee*]
illness	malattia [*mahlahtteeah*]
infection	infezione [*eenfaytseeohnay*]
injection	iniezione [*eenyaytseeohnay*]
intramuscolar injection	iniezione intramuscolare [*eenyaytseeohnay eentrahmooskohlahray*]
intravenous injection	iniezione endovenosa [*eenyaytseeohnay endohvaynohzah*]
lunatic asylum	manicomio [*mahneekohmeeoh*]
medical examination	visita medica [*veezetah maydeekah*]
medicine	medicina [*maydeecheenah*]
miscarriage	aborto [*ahborrtoh*]
nurse	infermiera [*eenfehrmeeayrah*]
obstetrician	ostetrico [*osstaytreekoh*]
oculist	oculista [*ohkooleestah*]
(to) operate	operare [*ohpayrahray*]
operation	operazione [*ohpayrahtseeohnay*]
operating table	letto operatorio [*lettoh ohpayrahtohreeoh*]
operating theatre	sala operatoria [*sahlah ohpayrahtohreeah*]
painkiller	calmante [*kahlmahntay*]
patient	malato [*mahlahtoh*]
physician	medico [*maydeekoh*]
pill	pillola [*peellohlah*]
plaster cast	ingessatura [*eendjayssahtoorah*]
prescription	ricetta [*reechettah*]
radiography	radiografia [*rahdeeohgrahfeeah*]
recovery	guarigione [*gwahreejohnay*]
Red Cross	Croce Rossa [*krohchay rosssah*]
remedy	rimedio [*reemaydeeoh*]
specialist physician	medico specialista [*maydeekoh spaychahleestah*]
stitches	punti [*poontee*]
stretcher	lettiga [*letteegah*]
surgeon	chirurgo [*keeroorgoh*]
surgery	ambulatorio [*ahmboolahtohreeoh*]
syringe	siringa [*seereenggah*]
treatment	cura [*koorah*]
vaccination	vaccinazione [*vahchcheenahtseeohnay*]
X-rays	raggi X [*rahdjee X*]

AT THE CHEMIST'S

Italian "farmacie" don't sell the great range of goods that can be found in Great Britain or in American drugstores (they don't sell photographic equipment or books); on the other hand, you can find there a lot of toiletries (see Perfumery). Farmacie are easily recognizable by a green or red cross ouside. A notice in the window indicates where the nearest all-night chemist's is.

antibiotics	antibiotici [*ahnteebeeohteechee*]
antiseptic cream	crema antisettica [*kraymah ahnteesaytteekah*]
aspirin	aspirina [*ahspeereenah*]
bandage	benda [*bayndah*]
band-aids	cerotti [*chayrottee*]
contraceptives	antifecondativi [*ahnteefaykohndahteevee*]
cotton wool	cotone idrofilo [*kohtohnay eedrohfeeloh*]
cough drops	pasticche per la tosse [*pahsteekkay pehr lah tosssay*]
disinfectant	disinfettante [*deezeenfettahntay*]
drops	gocce [*gohchchay*]
dummy	succhiotto [*sookkeeohttoh*]
ear drops	gocce per le orecchie [*gohchchay pehr lay ohreckkeeay*]
elastic bandage	benda elastica [*bendah aylahsteekah*]
eye drops	collirio [*kollleereeoh*]
feeding bottle	biberon [*beebayrohn*]
gauze	garza [*gahrdzah*]
insect repellent	crema contro gli insetti [*kraymah kontroh lyee eensettee*]
iodine	tintura di iodio [*teentoorah dee yohdeeoh*]
ice-bag	borsa del ghiaccio [*bohrsah dell gheeahchchoh*]
laxative	purgante [*poorgahntay*]
nappies	pannolini [*pahnnohleenee*]
peroxide	acqua ossigenata [*ahkkwah ossssejaynahtah*]
pill	pillola [*peellohlah*]
sanitary towels	assorbenti igienici [*ahssohrbayntee eejayneechee*]
sleeping pills	sonniferi [*sonnneefayree*]
suppository	supposta [*sooppoohstah*]
syringe	siringa [*seereengah*]
tablets	compresse [*kompresssay*]
thermometer	termometro [*tehrmohmaytroh*]
tranquillizers	calmanti [*kahlmahntee*]
vitamin pills	vitamine [*veetahmeenay*]

Where is the nearest all-night chemist's?	Dov'è la farmacia di turno più vicina? [*dohvay lah fahrmahcheeah dee toornoh peeoo veecheenah*?]
What time does the chemist's open?	A che ora apre la farmacia? [*ah kay ohray ahpray lah fahrmahcheeah*?]
I want some remedy for insect bites, sunburn and travel sickness	Desidero qualche rimedio contro le punture d'insetti, la scottatura solare e il mal d'auto [*dayzeedayroh kwahlkay reemaydeeoh kontroh lay poontooray deensayttee, lah skottahtoorah sohlahray ay eel mahl dowtoh*]
Can I get it without a prescription?	Posso avere questa medicina senza ricetta? [*posssoh ahvayray kwestah maydeechéenah sentsah reechettah*?]
External use only	Uso esterno [*oozoh essternoh*]
Poison!	Veleno! [*vaylaynoh*!]
Shake before using	Agitare prima dell'uso [*ahjeetahray preemah delloozoh*]
Must I take these pills before eating or after meals?	Devo prendere queste pillole prima o dopo i pasti? [*dayvoh prendayray kwesstay peellohlay preemah oh dohpoh ee pahstee*?]
I'd like a roll of plaster	Vorrei un rotolo di cerotto [*vorrayee oon rohtohloh dee chayrottoh*]

Xii SIGHTSEEING

CHURCH

abbey	abbazia [*ahbbahtseeah*]
aisle	navata [*nahvahtah*]
alms	elemosina [*aylaymohzeenah*]
altar	altare [*ahltahray*]
apse	abside [*ahbseeday*]
archbishop	arcivescovo [*archeevesskohvoh*]
atheist	ateo [*ahtayoh*]
baptistery	battistero [*bahtteestayroh*]
bell-tower	campanile [*kahmpahneelay*]
Bible	Bibbia [*beebeeah*]
bishop	vescovo [*vesskohvoh*]
(to) bless	benedire [*baynaydeeray*]
blessing	benedizione [*baynaydeetseeohnay*]
buddhist	buddhista [*booddeestah*]
candle	candela [*kahndaylah*]
cardinal	cardinale [*kahrdeenahlay*]
cathedral	cattedrale [*kahttaydrahlay*]
catholic	cattolico [*kahttohleekoh*]
cemetery	cimitero [*cheemeetayroh*]
chapel	cappella [*kahppelllah*]
Christ	Cristo [*kreestoh*]
(to) christen	battezzare [*bahttedzahray*]
christening	battesimo [*bahttayzemoh*]
christian	cristiano [*kreesteeahnoh*]
Christianity	cristianesimo [*kreesteeahnayzeemoh*]
choir	coro [*kohroh*]
clergyman	sacerdote [*sahchehrdohtay*]
cloister	chiostro [*keeohstroh*]
communion	comunione [*kohmooneeohnay*]
(to) confess	confessarsi [*konfesssahrsee*]
Confession	confessione [*konfessseeohnay*]
Confirmation	cresima [*krayzeemah*]
convent	convento [*konventoh*]
Cross	croce [*krohchay*]
Crucifix	Crocefisso [*krohchayfeessoh*]
cult	culto [*kooltoh*]
dome	cupola [*koopohlah*]
double window	bifora [*beefohrah*]
Easter	Pasqua [*pahskwah*]
extreme unction	estrema unzione [*esstraymah oontseeohnay*]
fresco	affresco [*ahffresskoh*]
funeral	corteo funebre [*korrtayoh foonaybray*]
glass window	vetrata [*vaytrahtah*]
God	Dio [*deeoh*]
Gospel	Vangelo [*vahndjayloh*]
gothic	gotico [*gohteekoh*]

grave	tomba [*tohmbah*]
graveyard	cimitero [*cheemeetayroh*]
hindu	indù [*eendoo*]
Holy service	funzione [*foontseeohnay*]
host	ostia [*ossteeah*]
Jesus	Gesù [*jayzoo*]
Jew	ebreo [*aybrayoh*]
kneeling-stool	inginocchiatoio [*eenjeenockkeeahtohyoh*]
Koran	Corano [*kohrahnoh*]
mass	messa [*messsah*]
mosaic	mosaico [*mohzaheekoh*]
mosque	moschea [*mosskayah*]
muslim	musulmano [*moozoolmahnoh*]
nave	navata [*nahvahtah*]
nun	suora [*sooohrah*]
orthodox	ortodosso [*ohrtohdossoh*]
parish	parrocchia [*pahrrockkeeah*]
pillar	pilastro [*peelahstroh*]
Pope	Papa [*pahpah*]
portal	portale [*porrtahlay*]
(to) pray	pregare [*praygahray*]
priest	prete [*praytay*]
protestant	protestante [*prohtaystahntay*]
pulpit	pulpito [*poolpeetoh*]
Rabbi	rabbino [*rahbbeenoh*]
sacrament	sacramento [*sahkrahmentoh*]
Sexton	sagrestano [*sahgresstahnoh*]
sacristy	sagrestia [*sahgressteeah*]
sanctuary	santuario [*sahntooahreeoh*]
spire	guglia [*goolyah*]
statue	statua [*stahtooah*]
style	stile [*steelay*]
Synagogue	sinagoga [*seenahgohgah*]
temple	tempio [*tempeeoh*]
vault	volta [*volltah*]

I'd like to visit the church	Vorrei visitare la chiesa [*vorrayee veezeetahray lah keeayzah*]
When does it open?	Quando apre? [*kwahndoh ahpray*?]
When does it close?	Quando chiude? [*kwahndoh keeooday*?]
How much is the entrance fee?	Quanto costa l'entrata? [*kwahntoh kohstah lentrahtah*?]
Is there any reduction for...?	C'è una riduzione per...? [*chay oonah reedootseeohnay pehr*...?]
Is there an English-speaking guide?	C'è una guida che parla inglese? [*chay oonah gweedah kay pahrlah eenglaysay*?]
Can I buy a catalogue?	Posso comprare un catalogo? [*posssoh komprahray oon kahtahlohgoh*?]

Is it allowed to go up the bell tower?	È possibile salire sul campanile? [*ay possseebeelay sahleeray sool kahmpahneeley*?]
Which way to go up?	Da che parte si sale? [*dah kay pahrtay see sahlay*?]
Is there a lift?	C'è un ascensore? [*chay oon ahshensohray*?]
Is it allowed to take pictures?	È permesso fare delle fotografie? [*ay pehrmesssoh fahray delllay fohtohgrahfeeay*?]

RELIGIOUS SERVICES

Is there a synagogue near here?	C'è una sinagoga qui vicino? [*chay oonah seenahgohgah kwee veecheenoh*?]
At what time is the service?	A che ora è la funzione? [*ah kay ohrah ay lah foontseohnay*?]
Where can I find a priest who speaks English?	Dove posso trovare un prete che parla inglese? [*dohvay posssoh trohvahray oon praytay kay pahrlah eenglaysay*?]
Can you tell me where there is a Catholic church?	Può dirmi dov'è una chiesa cattolica? [*poooh deermee dohvay oonah keeayzah kahttohleekah*?]
At what time are the Sunday services?	Qual è l'orario delle messe domenicali? [*kwahlay lohrahreeoh delllay messsay dohmayneekahlee*?]

Visitors to churches should always be suitably dressed, even if they are only there as tourists. Shorts, short skirts and even short sleeves are often considered disrespectful and visitors so attired could even find themselves being asked to leave.

POINTS OF INTEREST

abbey	abbazia [*ahbbahtseeah*]
age	età [*aytah*]
amphitheatre	anfiteatro [*ahnfeetayahtroh*]
ancient ruins	rovine antiche [*rohveenay ahnteekay*]
architecture	architettura [*ahrkeetehttoorah*]
balustrade	balaustra [*bahlowstrah*]
battlement	merlo [*mehrloh*]
bridge	ponte [*pohntay*]
building	costruzione [*kohstrootseeohnay*]
canal	canale [*cahnahlay*]
capital (of pillar)	capitello [*kahpeetellloh*]
castle	castello [*kahstellloh*]
catacombs	catacombe [*kahtahkohmbay*]
cathedral	cattedrale [*kahttaydrahlay*]
cemetery	cimitero [*cheemeetayroh*]
century	secolo [*saykohloh*]
chapel	cappella [*kahppelllah*]
convent	convento [*kohnvayntoh*]
courtyard	cortile [*korrteelay*]
decoration	decorazione [*daykohrahtseeohnay*]
draw-bridge	ponte levatoio [*pohntay layvahtohyoh*]
epoch	epoca [*aypohkah*]
exhibition	esposizione [*ayspohzeetseeohnay*]
façade	facciata [*fahchchahtah*]
fair	fiera [*feeayrah*]
fountain	fontana [*fohntahnah*]
furniture	mobili [*mohbeelee*]
glass	vetro [*vaytroh*]
harbour	porto [*pohrtoh*]
library	biblioteca [*beebleeohtaykah*]
light-house	faro [*fahroh*]
market	mercato [*mehrkahtoh*]
monastery	monastero [*mohnahstayroh*]
mosaic	mosaico [*mohzaheekoh*]
painting	pittura [*peettoorah*]
palace	palazzo [*pahlahtsoh*]
panorama	panorama [*pahnohrahmah*]
park	parco [*pahrkoh*]
period	periodo [*payreeohdoh*]
pillar	pilastro [*peelahstroh*]
porch	portico [*pohrteekoh*]
public gardens	giardini pubblici [*jahrdeenee poobbleechee*]
(to) rebuild	ricostruire [*reekosstrooeeray*]
(to) restore	restaurare [*resstowrahray*]
royal palace	palazzo reale [*pahlahtsoh rayahlay*]
shopping area	zona dei negozi [*zohnah dayee naygohtsee*]
statue	statua [*stahtooah*]

stadium	stadio [*stahdeeoh*]
style	stile [*steelay*]
stained-glass window	vetrata [*vaytrahtah*]
square	piazza [*peeahtsah*]
terrace	terrazza [*tehrrahtsah*]
tower	torre [*torrray*]
triumphal arch	arco di trionfo [*ahrkoh dee treeonfoh*]
view	vista [*veestah*]
visit	visita [*veezeetah*]
zoo	zoo [*dzohoh*]

Where's the tourist office?	Dov'è l'ufficio turistico? [*dohvay looffeechoh tooreesteekoh*?]
What are the main points of interest?	Quali sono i principali punti d'interesse? [*kwahlee sohnoh ee prencheepahlee poontee deentayresssay*?]
Can you recommend a sighseeing tour/an excursion?	Può consigliare un giro turistico/una gita? [*poooh konseelyahray oon jeeroh tooreesteekoh/oonah jeetah*?]
What's the point of departure?	Da dove si parte? [*dah dohvay see pahrtay*?]
How much does the tour cost?	Quanto costa il giro? [*kwahntoh kohstah eel jeeroh*?]
What time does the tour start?	A che ora inizia il giro? [*ah kay ohrah eeneetseeah eel jeeroh*?]
What time do we get back?	A che ora si ritorna? [*ah kay ohrah see reetohrnah*?]
Is there an English-speaking guide?	C'è una guida che parla inglese? [*chay oonah gweedah kay pahrlah eenglaysay*?]
I want to hire a private guide for half a day	Desidero avere una guida privata per mezza giornata [*dayzeedayroh ahvayray oonah gweedah preevahtah pehr medzah jorrnahtah*]
Where's the art gallery?	Dov'è la galleria d'arte? [*dohvay lah gahllayreeah dahrtay*?]
Can I buy a catalogue?	Posso comprare un catalogo? [*posssoh komprahray oon kahtahlohgoh*?]
We are interested in painting	Ci interessiamo di pittura [*chee eentayraysseeahmoh dee peettoorah*]
Are there any guided tours of the museum?	Ci sono delle visite guidate del museo? [*chee sohnoh delllay veezeetay gweedahtay dayl moozayoh*?]
Is there a reduction for groups?	C'è una riduzione per i gruppi? [*chay oonah reedootsyohnah pehr grooppee*?]

Xiii ENTERTAINMENTS AND SPORTS

CINEMA

Weekly entertainment guides are available at major newsstands, at the tourist offices and at the hotel reception in the main towns in Italy. Almost all foreign films are dubbed with no subtitles.

actor, actress	attore, attrice [*ahttohray, ahttreechay*]
adventure film	film d'avventura [*film dahvventoorah*]
balcony	galleria [*gahllayreeah*]
black and white film	film in bianco e nero [*film een beeahngkoh ay nayroh*]
cartoons	film a cartoni animati [*film ah kahrtohnee ahneemahtee*]
colour film	film a colori [*film ah kohlohree*]
comic film	film comico [*film kohmeekoh*]
criticism	critica [*kreeteekah*]
detective film	film giallo, poliziesco [*film jahlloh, pohleetseeayskoh*]
director	registra [*raydjeestah*]
documentary film	documentario [*dohkoomentahreeoh*]
dramatic film	film drammatico [*film drahmmahteekoh*]
first run, rerun	prima, seconda visione [*preemah, saykohndah veezeeohnay*]
first part, second part	primo, secondo tempo [*preemoh, saykohndoh tempoh*]
hard core film	film a luce rossa [*film ah loochay rosssah*]
horror film	film dell'orrore [*film dell'orrrohray*]
interval	intervallo [*eentehrvahlloh*]
main character, protagonist	protagonista [*prohtahgohneestah*]
musical film	film musicale [*film moozeekahlay*]
projection	proiezione [*prohyaytseeohnay*]
scene	scena [*shaynah*]
screen	schermo [*skerrmoh*]
show	spettacolo [*spettahkohloh*]
sound track	colonna sonora [*kohlonnah sohnohrah*]
stalls, pit	platea [*plahtayah*]
ticket	biglietto [*beelyettoh*]
title	titolo [*teetohloh*]
war film	film di guerra [*film dee gwehrrah*]
Where is the X cinema?	Dov'è il cinema X? [*dohvay eel cheenaymah?*]

What time is the last show?	A che ora è l'ultimo spettacolo? [*ah kay ohrah ay loolteemoh spettahkohloh*?]
Is the entrance forbidden to people under 14/18 years of age?	È vietato ai minori di 14/18 anni? [*ay veeaytahtoh ahee meenohree dee kwahttorrdeechee/deechottoh ahnnee*?]
What time does the show begin?	A che ora inizia lo spettacolo? [*ah kay ohrah eeneetseeah loh spettahkohloh*?]
Are there any seats for tonight?	Ci sono posti per questa sera? [*chee sohnoh posstee pehr kwesstah sayrah*?]
I'm sorry, we're sold out	Spiacente, tutto esaurito [*speeahchentay, toottoh ayzowreetoh*]
Can you recommend a good film?	Mi può consigliare un buon film? [*me poooh konseelyahray oon booohn film*?]
Who's in it?	Chi sono gli attori? [*kee sohnoh lyee ahttohree*?]

THEATRE

act	atto [*ahttoh*]
actor	attore [*ahttohray*]
actress	attrice [*ahttreechay*]
applaud	applaudire [*ahpplowdeeray*]
applause	applauso [*ahpplowzoh*]
ballet	balletto [*bahllayttoh*]
box in the Ist, 2nd row	palco di prima, seconda fila [*pahlkoh dee preemah, saykohndah feelah*]
character	personaggio [*pehrsohnahdjoh*]
concert	concerto [*konchehrtoh*]
(to) conduct	dirigere [*deereejayray*]
conductor (orchestra)	direttore d'orchestra [*deerayttohray d'orrkesstrah*]
costumes	costumi [*kohstoomee*]
curtain	sipario [*seepahreeoh*]
foot lights	luci della ribalta [*loochee delllah reebahltah*]
part, role	parte [*pahrtay*]
performance	esecuzione [*ayzaykootseeohnay*]
play	commedia [*kommaydeeah*]
scenery	scenografia [*shaynohgrahfeeah*]
seat	posto [*posstoh*]
stage	palcoscenico [*pahlkohshayneekoh*]
ticket	biglietto [*beelyettoh*]
usher, usherette	maschera [*mahskayrah*]

Where's the opera house?	Dov'è il teatro dell'opera? [*dohvay eel tayahtroh dellohpayrah?*]
What's on at the opera tonight?	Cosa danno all'opera questa sera? [*kohsah dahnnoh ahllohpayrah kwesstah sayrah?*]
I'd like to book a box	Vorrei prenotare un palco [*vorrayee praynohtahray oon pahlkoh*]

NIGHTLIFE

Ticket prices at discos and night clubs normally include the cost of your first drink.

Are there any good night clubs/discos?	Ci sono dei buoni locali notturni/delle buone discoteche? [*chee sohnoh dayee booohnee lohkahlee nottoornee/delllay booohnay deeskohtaykay*?]
Is there a floor show?	C'è il varietà? [*chay eel vahreeaytah*?]
How do we get to the casino?	Come si arriva al casinò? [*kohmay see ahrreevah ahl kahseenoh*?]
How much does it cost to get in?	Quanto costa il biglietto di entrata? [*kwahntoh kohstah eel beelyettoh dee entrahtah*?]
Is evening dress necessary?	È necessario l'abito da sera? [*ay naychesssahreeoh l'ahbeetoh dah sayrah*?]
We want to reserve two seats for tonight	Vogliamo prenotare due posti per stasera [*vollyahmoh praynohtahray dooay pohstee pehr stahsayrah*]
Where can we go to dance?	Dove possiamo andare per ballare? [*dohvay possseeahmoh ahndahray pehr ballahray*?]
Would you like to dance?	Vuole ballare [*vooohlay ballahray*?]

SPORTS

ALPINISM

alpine guide	guida alpina [*gweedah ahlpeenah*]
alpinism	alpinismo [*ahlpeeneesmoh*]
alpinist	alpinista [*ahlpeeneestah*]
bivouac	bivacco [*beevahkkoh*]
chasm	voragine [*vohrahjeenay*]
(to) climb	scalare [*skahlahray*]
climbing	scalata [*skahlahtah*]
climbing-boots	scarponi da montagna [*skahrpohnee dah montahnyah*]
clinkers	chiodi da scarponi [*keeohdee dah skahrpohnee*]
crevasse	crepaccio [*kraypahchchoh*]
glacier	ghiacciaio [*gheeahchchahyoh*]
hut	rifugio [*reefoojoh*]
ice-axe	piccozza [*peekkohtzah*]
rock	roccia [*rohchchah*]
rope	corda [*korrdah*]
roped party	cordata [*korrdahtah*]
rucksack	sacco da montagna [*sahkkoh dah montahnyah*]
sleeping-bag	sacco a pelo [*sahkkoh ah payloh*]
snow-goggles	occhiali da neve [*ockkeeahlee dah nayvay*]

ATHLETICS

athlete	atleta [*ahtlaytah*]
athletics	atletica [*ahtlayteekah*]
gymnasium	palestra [*pahlesstrah*]
gymnastic	ginnastica [*jeennahsteekah*]
high jump	salto in alto [*sahltoh een ahltoh*]
jump	salto [*sahltoh*]
long jump	salto in lungo [*sahltoh een loonggoh*]
marathon	maratona [*mahrahtohnah*]
pole jump	salto con l'asta [*sahltoh kon lahstah*]
runner	corridore [*korrreedohray*]
running	corsa [*korrsah*]
sprinter	corridore di breve distanza [*korrreedohray dee brayvay deestahntsah*]
throwing the discus	lancio del disco [*lahnchoh dell deeskoh*]
throwing the hammer	lancio del martello [*lahnchoh dell mahrtellloh*]
throwing the javelin	lancio del giavellotto [*lahnchoh dell jahvellottoh*]

throwing the weight	lancio del peso [*lahnchoh dell paysoh*]
weight-lifting	sollevamento pesi [*solllayvahmentoh paysee*]

BASEBALL

bases	angoli del campo [*ahnggohlee dell kahmpoh*]
bat	mazza [*mahtzah*]
batter	battitore [*bahtteetohray*]
catcher	prenditore [*prendeetohray*]
diamond	campo [*kahmpoh*]
fair hit	colpo giusto [*kohlpoh joostoh*]
foul hit	colpo errato [*kohlpoh ehrrahtoh*]
pitcher	lanciatore [*lahnchahtohray*]
team	squadra [*skwahdrah*]
umpire	arbitro [*ahrbeetroh*]

BOATING

boating	canottaggio [*khanottahjoh*]
canoe	canoa [*kahnohah*]
cox	timoniere [*teemohneeayray*]
keel	chiglia [*keelyah*]
oar	remo [*raymoh*]
oarsman	vogatore [*vohgahtohray*]
outboard motor-boat	fuoribordo [*foohoreeborrdoh*]
paddle	pagaia [*pahgaheeah*]
regatta	regata [*raygahtah*]
(to) row	remare [*raymahray*]
rowlock	scalmo [*skahlmoh*]
rudder	timone [*teemohnay*]
sliding seat	sedile scorrevole [*saydeelay skorrayvohlay*]
stretcher	poggiapiedi [*pohdjahpeeaydee*]
the pair oar-boat without/with coxswain	due senza/con timoniere [*dooay sentsah/kon teemohneeayray*]

BOXING

bantam-weight	peso gallo [*paysoh gahlloh*]
boxer	pugile [*poojeelay*]
boxing	pugilato [*poojeelahtoh*]
boxing glove	guantone [*gwahntohnay*]
boxing match	incontro [*eekontroh*]
blow	colpo [*kohlpoh*]
corner	angolo [*ahngohloh*]
disqualified	squalificato [*skwahleefeekahtoh*]

fly weight	peso mosca [*paysoh mohskah*]
hook	gancio [*gahncheeoh*]
k.o. = knock out (technical k.o.)	k.o. tecnico [*kahppah o taykneekoh*]
low blow	colpo basso [*kohlpoh bahssoh*]
punch	colpo [*kohlpoh*]
(to) receive blows	incassare [*eenkahssahray*]
referee	arbitro [*ahrbeetroh*]
rope	corda [*kohrdah*]
straight	diretto [*deerayttoh*]
(to) win by points	battere ai punti [*bahttayray ahee poontee*]

CYCLING

bell	campanello [*kahmpahnellloh*]
bicycle	bicicletta [*beecheeklettah*]
brake	freno [*fraynoh*]
chain	catena [*kahtaynah*]
cycling	ciclismo [*cheekleesmoh*]
cyclist	ciclista [*cheekleestah*]
descent	discesa [*deeshaysah*]
frame	telaio [*taylaheeoh*]
front wheel	ruota anteriore [*roohotah ahntayreeohray*]
handle	manopola [*mahnohpohlah*]
handlebar	manubrio [*mahnoobreeoh*]
handlebar stem	sterzo [*stehrtzoh*]
high speed	fuga [*foogah*]
inner tube	camera d'aria [*kahmayrah dahreeah*]
lamp	fanale [*fahnahlay*]
mudguard	parafango [*pahrahfahngoh*]
pedal	pedale [*paydahlay*]
pink jersey (first place in the tour of Italy)	maglia rosa [*mahlyah rohzah*]
pump	pompa [*pohmpah*]
pursuit	inseguimento [*eensaygweementoh*]
racer	corridore [*korreedohray*]
race track	pista [*peestah*]
racing bicycle	bicicletta da corsa [*beecheeklettah dah kohrsah*]
rear wheel	ruota posteriore [*rooohtah posstayreeohray*]
rim	cerchione [*chehrkeeohnay*]
speedometer	contachilometri [*kohntahkeelohmaytree*]
spokes	raggi [*rahdjee*]
(to) spring	scattare [*skahttahray*]
supporting rider	gregario [*graygahreeoh*]
time lap	tappa a cronometro [*tahppah ah krohnohmaytroh*]
tyres	gomme [*gohmmay*]

variable gear	cambio di velocità [*kahmbeeoh dee vaylohcheetah*]
wheel	ruota [*rooohtah*]
winner of the stage	vincitore di tappa [*veencheetohray dee tahppah*]

FENCING

a feint	finta [*feentah*]
assault	assalto [*ahssahltoh*]
(to) attack	attaccare [*ahttahkkahray*]
(to) fence	tirare di scherma [*teerahray dee skehrmah*]
fencer	schermitore [*skehrmeetohray*]
fencing	scherma [*skehrmah*]
fencing glove	guanto da scherma [*gwahntoh dah skehrmah*]
fencing hall	sala di scherma [*sahlah dee skehrmah*]
fencing mask	maschera [*mahskayrah*]
fencing master	maestro di scherma [*mahesstroh dee skehrmah*]
fending off a blow	fendente [*fendayntay*]
foil	fioretto [*feeohrayttoh*]
foilist	fiorettista [*feeohraytteestah*]
in position of guard	in guardia [*een gwahrdeeah*]
(to) parry	parare [*pahrahray*]
parry	parata [*pahrahtah*]
sabre	sciabola [*shahbohlah*]
salute	posizione di saluto [*pohzeetseeohnay dee sahlootoh*]
sword	spada [*spahdah*]
thrust	stoccata [*stockkahtah*]

FISHING

angler	pescatore con la lenza [*pesskahtohray kon lah lentzah*]
barb	uncino dell'amo [*ooncheenoh dellahmoh*]
bait	esca [*esskah*]
(to) fish with rod and reel	pescare con canna da mulinello [*pesskahray kon kahnnah dah mooleenellloh*]
fishing	pesca [*pesskah*]
fishing basket	cestello [*chesstellloh*]
float	galleggiante [*gahllaydjahntay*]
hook	amo [*ahmoh*]
line	lenza [*lentzah*]
net	rete [*raytay*]
rod	canna da pesca [*kahnnah dah pesskah*]

FOOTBALL (SOCCER)

ball	palla [*pahllah*]
captain	capitano [*kahpeetahnoh*]
centre-forward	centro avanti [*chentroh ahvahntee*]
championship	campionato [*kahmpeeohnahtoh*]
corner	angolo [*ahnggohloh*]
field	campo [*kahmpoh*]
football	calcio [*kahlchoh*]
forwards	attaccanti [*ahttahkkahntee*]
free kick	calcio di punizione [*kahlchoh dee pooneetseeohnay*]
game	partita [*pahrteetah*]
goal	porta [*pohrtah*]
goal keeper	portiere [*porrteeayray*]
ground	campo [*kahmpoh*]
half-back	mediano [*maydeeahnoh*]
hands!	fallo di mano [*fahlloh dee mahnoh*]
header	colpo di testa [*kohlpoh dee taystah*]
inside right/left	mezz'ala destra/sinistra [*medzahlah desstrah/seeneestrah*]
interval	intervallo [*eentehrvahllloh*]
left wing	ala sinistra [*ahlah seeneestrah*]
linesmen	guardalinee [*gwahrdahleenayay*]
net	rete [*raytay*]
offside	fuori gioco [*fooohree jooohkoh*]
out	fallo laterale [*fahllloh lahtayrahlay*]
overtime periods	tempi supplementari [*taympee sooppplaymentahree*]
penalty	punizione [*pooneetseeohnay*]
penalty area	area di rigore [*ahrayah dee reegohray*]
penalty kick	calcio di rigore [*kahlchoh dee reegohray*]
(to) play at home	giocare in casa [*johkahray een kahsah*]
(to) play away	giocare in trasferta [*johkahray een trahsfehrtah*]
player	giocatore [*johkahtohray*]
referee	arbitro [*ahrbeetroh*]
right wing	ala destra [*ahlah desstrah*]
soccer	calcio [*kahlchoh*]
stadium	stadio [*stahdeeoh*]
stand	tribuna [*treeboonah*]
(to) support a team	fare il tifo per... [*fahray eel teefoh pehr...*]
sweeper	(giocatore) libero [*johkahtohray leebayroh*]
terrace	gradinata [*grahdeenahtah*]
trainer	allenatore [*ahllaynahtohray*]
throw in	rimessa laterale [*reemaysssah lahtayrahlay*]
warning	ammonizione [*ahmmmohneetseeohnay*]

GLIDING

(to) glide	planare [*plahnahray*]
gliding	volo a vela [*vohloh ah vaylah*]
glider	aliante [*ahleeahntay*]

GOLF

bunker	terreno difficile [*tehrraynoh deeffeecheelay*]
caddie	ragazzo porta bastoni [*rahgahtsoh porrtah bahstohnee*]
club	bastone da golf [*bahstohnay dah golf*]
golf bag	sacco porta bastoni [*sahkkoh porrtah bahstohnee*]
golfer	giocatore [*johkahtohray*]
golf links	campo di golf [*kahmpoh dee golf*]
hole	buca [*bookah*]
movable flag	bandierina movibile [*bahndeeayreenah mohveebeelay*]
stroke	colpo [*kohlpoh*]

GYMNASTICS

asymmetric parallel bars	parallele asimmetriche [*pahrahlllaylay ahseemmmaytreekay*]
balancing form	asse di equilibrio [*ahssay dee aykweeleebreeoh*]
floor exercise	corpo libero [*kohrpoh leebayroh*]
gymnastic	ginnastica da palestra [*jeennahsteekah dah pahlestrah*]
horizontal bar	sbarra fissa [*sbahrrah feessah*]
parallel bars	parallele [*pahrahlllaylay*]
rings	anelli [*ahnelllee*]
vaulting horse	cavallo [*kahvahlloh*]
wall bars	spalliere [*spahllleeayray*]

MOTORING

autodrome	autodromo [*owtohdrohmoh*]
car	automobile [*owtohmohbeelay*]
engine	motore [*mohtohray*]
motorcar race	corsa automobilistica [*kohrsah owtohmohbeeleesteekah*]
motoring	automobilismo [*owtohmohbeeleezmoh*]
race-car	automobile da corsa [*owtohmohbeelay dah kohrsah*]
racer	corridore [*kohrreedohray*]
race on the road	corsa su strada [*kohrsah soo strahdah*]
race on the track	corsa su pista [*kohrsah soo peestah*]

RIDING

(to) bet	scommettere [*skommettayray*]
bet	scommessa [*skommesssah*]
bit	morso [*mohrsoh*]
blinkers	paraocchi [*pahrahockkee*]
bridle	briglia [*breelyah*]
colt	puledro [*poolaydroh*]
currycomb	striglia [*streelyah*]
ditch	fosso [*fosssoh*]
favourite	favorito [*fahvohreetoh*]
fence	siepe [*seeaypay*]
gallop race	corsa al galoppo [*kohrsah ahl gahloppoh*]
hippodrome	ippodromo [*eeppohdrohmoh*]
horse	cavallo [*kahvahlloh*]
horse-race	corsa di cavalli [*korsah dee kahvahllee*]
jockey	fantino [*fahnteenoh*]
jump	salto [*sahltoh*]
mane	criniera [*kreeneeayrah*]
mare	cavalla [*kahvahllah*]
number board	quadro degli arrivi [*kwahdroh daylyee ahrreevee*]
obstacles	ostacoli [*ohstahkohlee*]
pace	andatura [*ahndahtoorah*]
reins	redini [*raydeenee*]
(to) ride	cavalcare [*kahvahlkahray*]
riding	equitazione [*aykweetahtseeohnay*]
riding-school	maneggio [*mahnaydjoh*]
saddle	sella [*selllah*]
spurs	speroni [*spayrohnee*]
stable	stalla [*stahllah*]
starting gate	partenza [*pahrtentsah*]
steeple chase	corsa a ostacoli [*kohrsah ah ohstahkohlee*]
stirrup	staffa [*stahffah*]
tail	coda [*kohdah*]
totalizor	totalizzatore [*tohtahleetsahtohray*]
track	pista [*peestah*]
trot	trotto [*trottoh*]
trotting match	corsa al trotto [*kohrsah ahl trottoh*]
walk	passo [*pahssoh*]
whip	frusta [*froostah*]
winner	vincente [*veenchayntay*]
winning post	traguardo [*trahgwahrdoh*]

SAILING

bow	prua [*prooah*]
drift	deriva [*dayreevah*]
jib	fiocco [*feeockkoh*]

regatta	regata [*raygahtah*]
rudder	timone [*teemohnay*]
sailing	vela [*vaylay*]
sailing-boat	barca a vela [*bahrkah ah vaylah*]
spanker	randa [*rahndah*]
spanker-boom	scotta [*skohttah*]
stern	poppa [*poppah*]

SHOOTING AND TARGET SHOOTING

(to) aim the gun	puntare il fucile [*poontahray eel foocheelay*]
archery	tiro con l'arco [*teeroh kon lahrkoh*]
cartridge	cartuccia [*kahrtoochchah*]
double-barelled gun	doppietta [*dohppeeaytttah*]
game	selvaggina [*sellvahdjeenah*]
game-pouch	carniere [*kahrneeayray*]
game preserve	riserva di caccia [*reesehrvay dee kahchchah*]
(to) go hunting	andare a caccia [*ahndahray ah kahchchah*]
gun	fucile [*foocheelay*]
gun powder	polvere da sparo [*pollvayray dah spahroh*]
(to) hit the bull's eye	centrare il bersaglio [*chentrahray eel behrsahlyoh*]
hound	cane da caccia [*kahnay dah kahchchah*]
hunter	cacciatore [*kahchchahtohray*]
hunting knife	coltello da caccia [*kolltellloh dah kahchchah*]
hunting permit	permesso di caccia [*pehrmesssoh dee kahchchah*]
(to) load a gun	caricare un fucile [*kahreekahray oon foocheelay*]
migrant game	selvaggina migratoria [*sellvahdjeenah meegrahtohreeah*]
no hunting allowed	divieto di caccia [*deeveeaytoh dee kahchchah*]
pack of hounds	muta di cani [*mootah dee kahnee*]
pistol	pistola [*peestohlah*]
(to) poach	cacciare di frodo [*kahchchahray dee frohdoh*]
private hunting	caccia riservata [*kahchchah reeserhrvahtah*]
protected game	selvaggina protetta [*sellvahdjeenah prohtaytttah*]
rifle	carabina [*kahrahbeenah*]
(to) shoot at the target	tirare a segno [*teerahray ah saynyoh*]
shooting	caccia [*kahchchah*]
shooting dog	cane da caccia [*kahnay dah kahchchah*]

shooting licence	licenza di caccia [*leechentzah dee kahchchah*]
shotgun	fucile da caccia [*foocheelay dah kahchchah*]
small shots	pallini [*pahlleenee*]
(to) stalk	mettersi alla posta [*mettayrsee ahllah pohsstah*]
(to) take aim	mirare [*meerahray*]
target	bersaglio [*behrsahlyoh*]
target shooting	tiro a segno [*teeroh ah saynyoh*]
trap-shooting	tiro al piattello [*teeroh ahl peeahttellloh*]

SKATING

roller-skates	pattini a rotelle [*pahtteenee ah rohtayllay*]
(to) skate	pattinare [*pahtteenahray*]
skates	pattini [*pahtteenee*]
skating	pattinaggio [*pahtteenahdjoh*]
skating-rink	pista di pattinaggio [*peestah dee pahtteenahdjoh*]

SKI

binding	attacco [*ahttahkkoh*]
(to) ski	sciare [*sheeahray*]
ski boots	scarponi [*skahrpohnee*]
skier	sciatore [*sheeahtohray*]
ski	sci [*shee*]
ski-runs	piste [*peestay*]
ski-wax	sciolina [*sheeohleenah*]
stick	racchetta [*rahkkettah*]
water-skiing	sci d'acqua [*shee dahkkwah*]
wind jacket	giacca a vento [*jahkkah ah ventoh*]

SWIMMING

back stroke	nuoto a dorso [*nooohtoh ah dorrsoh*]
bathing hut	cabina [*kahbeenah*]
breast stroke	nuoto a rana [*nooohtoh ah rahnah*]
butterfly stroke	nuoto a farfalla [*nooohtoh ah fahrfahlllah*]
crawl	nuoto a bracciate [*nooohtoh ah brahchchahtay*]
deck-chair	sedia a sdraio [*saydeeah ah sdrahyoh*]
(to) dive	tuffarsi [*tooffahrsee*]
diving board	trampolino [*trahmpohleenoh*]
dolphin stroke	nuoto a delfino [*nooohtoh ah dellfeenoh*]

free-style swimming	nuoto a stile libero [*nooohtoh ah steelay leebayroh*]
no swimming	divieto di balneazione [*deeveeaytoh dee bahlnayahtseeohnay*]
(to) swim	nuotare [*nooohtahray*]
swimmer	nuotatore [*nooohtahtohray*]
swimming	nuoto [*nooohtoh*]
swimming-pool	piscina [*peesheenah*]
swimming race	gara di nuoto [*gahrah dee nooohtoh*]

TABLE TENNIS

ball	pallina [*pahlleenah*]
bat	racchetta [*rahkkettah*]
game	partita [*pahrteetah*]
net	rete [*raytay*]
ping-pong table	tavolo [*tahvohloh*]
points	punteggio [*poontaydjoh*]

TENNIS

backhand stroke	rovescio [*rohvayshoh*]
ball	palla [*pahllah*]
ball-boy	raccattapalle [*rahkkkahtttahpahllay*]
base line	linea di fondo [*leenayah dee fohndoh*]
doubles	doppio [*doppeeoh*]
fault	fallo [*fahlloh*]
game	gioco [*jooohkoh*]
net	rete [*raytay*]
racket	racchetta [*rahkkettah*]
return stroke	colpo di ritorno [*kohlpoh dee reetorrnoh*]
service	battuta [*bahtttootah*]
set	set
single match	singolo [*seenggohloh*]
smash	schiacciata [*skeeahchcheeahtah*]
tennis court	campo da tennis [*kahmpoh dah tennis*]
tennis tournament	torneo [*torrnayoh*]
tram lines	corridoio [*kohrrreedohyoh*]

I'd like to see a football match (soccer)	Vorrei vedere una partita di calcio [*vorrayee vaydayray oonah pahrteetah dee kahlchoh*]
Can you get me a ticket?	Mi può procurare un biglietto? [*mee poooh prohkoorahray oon beelyettoh*?]
Where are the tennis courts?	Dove sono i campi da tennis? [*dohvay sohnoh ee kahmpee dah tennis*?]
What's the charge per hour?	Qual è il prezzo per un'ora? [*kwahlay eel pretsoh pehr oon ohrah*?]
Can I rent rackets?	Posso noleggiare le racchette? [*posssoh nohlaydjahray lay rahkkettay*?]

Is there a swimming pool here?	C'è una piscina qui? [*chay oonah peesheenah kwee*?]
Is there a sand beach?	C'è una spiaggia di sabbia? [*chay oonah speeahdjah dee sahbbeeah*?]
I want to hire a sunshade umbrella	Desidero noleggiare un ombrellone [*dayzeedayroh nohlaydjahray oon ombrelllohnay*]
Is there a lifeguard?	C'è un bagnino? [*chay oon bahnyeenoh*?]
Are there any ski-runs for beginners?	Ci sono piste per principianti? [*chee sohnoh peestay pehr preencheepeeahntee*?]
Are there ski lifts?	Ci sono sciovie? [*chee sohnoh sheeohveeay*?]
I want to hire skiing equipment	Desidero noleggiare una tenuta di sci [*dayzeedayroh nohlaydjahray oonah taynootah dah shee*]

XiV USEFUL ABBREVIATIONS

AA.RR. biglietti di andata e ritorno	**return tickets**
A.A.T. Azienda Autonoma di Soggiorno	**local tourist board**
a.C. avanti Cristo	**B.C.**
A.C.I. Automobile Club d'Italia	**Italian Automobile Association**
A.G. Alberghi per la Gioventù	**Youth Hostels**
A.G.I.P. Azienda Generale Italiana Petroli	**National Italian Oil Company**
alt. altezza, altitudine	**height, altitude**
A.N.S.A. Agenzia Nazionale Stampa Associata	**Italian Associated Press Agency**
A.T.M. Azienda Tranviaria Municipale	**City Rapid Transit Board**
A.V.I.S. Associazione Volontari Italiani del Sangue	**Association of Voluntary Italian Blood-Donors**
B.I. Banca d'Italia	**Bank of Italy**
B.U. Bollettino Ufficiale	**Official Gazette**
C.A.I. Club Alpino Italiano	**Italian Alpine Club**
C.E.E. Comunità Economica Europea	**European Economic Community (E.E.C.)**
C.I.G.A. Compagnia Italiana dei Grandi Alberghi	**Italian Great Hotels Company**
C.I.T. Compagnia Italiana del Turismo	**Italian Travel Bureau**
cm centimetro	**centimetre (cm)**
c.m. corrente mese	**instant (inst)**
C.O.N.I. Comitato Olimpico Nazionale Italiano	**Italian Committee for the Olympic Games**
C.P. casella postale	**Post (Office) Box**
C.R.I. Croce Rossa Italiana	**Italian Red Cross**
c.so corso	**Avenue (av.)**
d.C. dopo Cristo	**Anno Domini (A.D.)**
ecc. eccetera	**et cetera, and so on**
E.I. Esercito Italiano	**Italian Army**
E.N.E.L. Ente Nazionale per l'Energia Elettrica	**National Board for Electric Power**

E.N.I.T. Ente Nazionale Italiano per il Turismo	**Italian State Tourist Office**
E.N.P.A. Ente Nazionale Protezione Animali	**National Society for the Prevention of Cruelty to Animals**
es. esempio	**example (ex)**
E.U.R. Esposizione Universale di Roma	**Roman Universal Exhibition**
FF.SS. Ferrovie dello Stato	**(Italian) State Railways**
F.I.A.T. Fabbrica Italiana Automobili Torino	**Italian Motor Works in Turin**
I.N.A.M. Istituto Nazionale Assicurazione Malattie	**National Health Insurance Board**
I.N.P.S. Istituto Nazionale di Previdenza Sociale	**National Organization of Social Insurance**
I.V.A. Imposta sul Valore Aggiunto	**Value-added Tax (V.A.T.)**
Lit. lire italiane	**Italian Lire**
lit. litro	**litre**
m metro	**metre**
M. Monte	**Mount (Mt.)**
M.E.C. Mercato Europeo Comune	**European Common Market (E.C.M.)**
mitt. (sulle buste) mittente	**sender, from**
N.U. Nazioni Unite	**United Nations**
O.N.U. Organizzazione delle Nazioni Unite	**United Nation Organization (U.N.O.)**
p. piazza; pagina	**square; page**
P.E. Parlamento Europeo	**European Parliament**
P.I. Pubblica Istruzione	**Public Education**
POLFER Polizia Ferroviaria	**Railway Police**
POLSTRADA Polizia Stradale	**Highway Police**
PP.TT. Poste e Telecomunicazioni	**Post Telephone and Telegraph Services**
P.T. Poste e Telegrafi	**Post and Telegraph Service**
p.za, piazza	**square**
R.A.I.-T.V. Radio Audizioni Italiane e Televisione	**Italian TV and Broadcasting Corporation**
S.C.V. Stato della Città del Vaticano	**Vatican City**

Sig. Signor	**Mister (Mr)**
Sig.a Signora	**Mistress (Mrs)**
Sigg. Signori	**Messieurs (Messrs)**
Sig.na Signorina	**Miss**
S.I.P. Società Italiana per l'Esercizio Telefonico	**Italian Stateowned Telephone Company**
T.C.I. Touring Club Italiano	**Italian Touring Club**
TOTIP Totalizzatore Ippico	**Horse-Race Pools**
TOTOCALCIO Totalizzatore del (gioco del) Calcio	**Football Pools**
VV.UU. Vigili Urbani	**Traffic Police**

XV EMERGENCY TELEPHONE NUMBERS

113	Police-all-purpose emergency number
112	Carabinieri
116	Road Assistance
115	Fire
5100	Ambulance (Red Cross)
5544	Highway patrol

XVi SHORT GRAMMAR

ARTICLES

There are two genders in Italian: masculine and feminine.

DEFINITE ARTICLE (the)

The definite article must agree in gender and number with the noun it precedes.

Il [*eel*]	before masculine singular nouns. Ex: il treno = the train
La [*lah*]	before feminine singular nouns. Ex: la casa = the house
L'	before either masculine or feminine singular nouns beginning with a vowel. Ex: l'uomo = the man, l'attrice = the actress
Lo [*loh*]	before masculine singular nouns which begin with *z* or *s* followed by a consonant. Ex: lo zio = the uncle, lo sposo = the bridegroom
I [*ee*]	before masculine plural nouns. Ex: i treni = the trains
Le [*lay*]	before feminine plural nouns. Ex: le donne = the women
Gli [*lyee*]	before masculine plural nouns which begin with a vowel, *z* or *s* followed by a consonant. Ex: gli amici = the friends, gli sposi = the bridegrooms

INDEFINITE ARTICLE (a/an)

The indefinite article also agrees in number and gender with the noun it precedes.

Un [*oon*]	before a masculine noun. Ex: un uomo = a man.
Uno [*oonoh*]	before a masculine noun which begins with *z* or *s* followed by a consonant. Ex: uno specchio = a mirror
Una [*oonah*]	before a feminine noun. Ex: una strada = a street
Un' [*oon*]	before a feminine noun which begins with a vowel. Ex: un'amica = a girl friend

PLURAL OF NOUNS

Nouns ending in *o* are generally masculine. To form the plural the final vowel is changed to *i*.

Ex: libro = book libri = books

Nouns ending in *a* are generally feminine. To form the plural the final vowel is changed to *e*.

Ex: porta = door porte = doors

Nouns ending in *e* have no rule as to gender. Plurals are formed by changing the *e* to *i*.

Ex: notte = night notti = nights

ADJECTIVES

Adjectives agree in number and gender with the nouns they qualify, and generally follow the noun.
When an adjective ends in *o* in the masculine, this changes to *a* in the feminine. Other adjectives do not change.

Ex: masculine	bello (beautiful)	freddo (cold)	grande (big)
feminine	bella	fredda	grande
plural	belle/belli	fredde/freddi	grandi

POSSESSIVE ADJECTIVES AND PRONOUNS

Possessive adjectives and pronouns are identical.
Possessive adjectives and pronouns in Italian agree in gender and number *with the thing possessed*, and not with the possessor as in English. The definite article is used with possessive adjectives and pronouns in Italian. Ex: my book = il mio libro.

	MASCULINE		FEMININE	
	sing.	*plur.*	*sing.*	*plur.*
my, mine	il mio [*eel meeoh*]	i miei [*ee meeayee*]	la mia [*lah meeah*]	le mie [*lay meeay*]
your, yours **(familiar)**	il tuo [*eel toooh*]	i tuoi [*ee tooohee*]	la tua [*lah tooah*]	le tue [*lay tooay*]
his, her, hers, its	il suo [*eel soooh*]	i suoi [*ee sooohee*]	la sua [*lah sooah*]	le sue [*lay sooay*]
our, ours	il nostro [*eel nosstroh*]	i nostri [*ee nosstree*]	la nostra [*lah nosstrah*]	le nostre [*lay nosstray*]
your, yours	il vostro [*eel vosstroh*]	i vostri [*ee vosstree*]	la vostra [*lah vosstrah*]	le vostre [*lay vosstray*]
their, theirs	il loro [*eel lohroh*]	i loro [*ee lohroh*]	la loro [*lah lohroh*]	le loro [*lay lohroh*]
your, yours **(formal)**	il loro	i loro	la loro	le loro

DEMONSTRATIVE ADJECTIVES AND PRONOUNS

this	questo/questa [*kwesstoh/kwesstah*] contracted to *quest'* before a vowel
these	questi/queste [*kwesstee/kwesstay*] no contraction
that	quello/quel/quella/quell' [*kwelloh/kwell/kwellah/kwell*]
those	quegli/quei/quelle [*kwaylyee/kwayee/kwellay*]

PERSONAL PRONOUNS

SUBJECT	CONJUNCTIVE		REFLEXIVE OBJECT	DISJUNCTIVE Used after prepositions, in comparison, for special emphasis
	direct object	*indirect object*		
io = I [*eeoh*]	mi = me [*mee*]	mi = to me [*mee*]	mi = myself [*mee*]	me = I, me [*meh*]
tu [*too*] = thou / you (informal)	ti [*tee*] = thee / you	ti [*tee*] = to thee / to you	ti [*tee*] = thyself / yourself	te [*teh*] = thou, thee / you
egli = he [*aylyee*]	lo [*loh*] = him / it (m.)	gli [*lyee*] = to him / to it (m.)		lui [*looee*] = he, him
ella = she [*eellah*]			si [*see*] = himself / herself / itself / yourself / oneself	lei [*layee*] = she, her / you / (m. or f. sing.)
esso = it (m.) [*essoh*]				
essa = it (f.) [*essah*]	la [*lah*] = her / it (f.)	le [*lay*] = to her / to it (f.)		
lei = you [*layee*] (formal)				

<table>
<tr><th rowspan="2">SUBJECT</th><th colspan="2">CONJUNCTIVE</th><th rowspan="2">REFLEXIVE OBJECT</th><th rowspan="2">DISJUNCTIVE
Used after prepositions, in comparison, for special emphasis</th></tr>
<tr><th>direct object</th><th>indirect object</th></tr>
<tr><td>noi = we
[nohee]</td><td>ci = us
[chee]</td><td>ci = to us
[chee]</td><td>ci = ourselves
[chee]</td><td>noi = we, us
[nohee]</td></tr>
<tr><td></td><td></td><td></td><td></td><td></td></tr>
<tr><td>voi = you
[voyee]</td><td>vi = you
[vee]</td><td>vi = to you
[vee]</td><td>vi = yourselves
[vee]</td><td>voi = you
[voyee]</td></tr>
<tr><td>essi = they (m.)
[essee]</td><td>li = { them (m.) / you (m.) }
[lee]</td><td rowspan="3">loro = { to them (m. or f.) / to you (m. or f.) }
[lohroh]</td><td rowspan="3">si = { themselves / yourselves }
[see]</td><td rowspan="3">loro = { they, them / you (m. or f. pl.) }
[lohroh]</td></tr>
<tr><td>esse = they (f.)
[essah]</td><td rowspan="2">le = { them (f.) / you (f.) }
[lay]</td></tr>
<tr><td>loro = you
[lohroh] (pl. formal)</td></tr>
</table>

NOTES ON SUBJECT PRONOUNS

The 1st person singular is not written with a capital letter in Italian as in English.
The 2nd person singular in Italian, *tu*, is only used when speaking to children, relative and close friends. In all other cases *lei* must be used, with the verb ending as for the 3rd person singular.
The nominative pronoun is generally omitted in Italian, except when the verb alone is not sufficient to indicate the meaning, or when special emphasis is needed.

Examples of Personal Pronouns

io lo (la) vedo	I see him (her)
gli (le) scriverò	I shall write to him (her)

It will be seen that Conjunctive Object Pronouns generally precede the Verb of which they are the object. However, with the Infinitive, the Present Participle, or *ecco* (here is/are) they are placed after, as part of the same word.

Ex:

eccolo/la	here he/she is
vorrei vederlo/a	I would like to see him/her
parlandola si impara una lingua	by speaking it, one learns a language

When the Conjunctive Pronoun is added to the Infinitive, the last vowel of the latter must first be dropped.

Examples of Disjunctive Personal Pronouns

Il bambino è con lui/lei	The boy is with him/her
Luisa è più alta di me	Louisa is taller than me

VERBS

Essere [*essayray*] **to be**	**Avere** [*ahvayray*] **to have**
PRESENT INDICATIVE	
io sono [*sohnoh*] **I am**	io ho [*oh*] **I have**
tu sei [*sayee*]	tu hai [*ahee*]
egli è [*eh*]	egli ha [*ah*]
noi siamo [*syahmoh*]	noi abbiamo [*ahbyahmoh*]
voi siete [*syaytay*]	voi avete [*ahvaytay*]
essi sono [*sohnoh*]	essi hanno [*ahnnoh*]
IMPERFECT	
io ero [*ayroh*] **I was**	io avevo [*ahvayvoh*] **I had**
tu eri [*ayree*]	tu avevi [*ahvayvee*]
egli era [*ayrah*]	egli aveva [*ahvayvah*]
noi eravamo [*ayrahvahmoh*]	noi avevamo [*ahvayvahmoh*]
voi eravate [*ayrahvahtay*]	voi avevate [*ahvayvahtay*]
essi erano [*ayrahnoh*]	essi avevano [*ahvayvahnoh*]
SIMPLE PAST	
io fui [*fooee*] **I was**	io ebbi [*aybee*] **I had**
tu fosti [*fosstee*]	tu avesti [*ahvesstee*]
egli fu [*foo*]	egli ebbe [*aybbay*]
noi fummo [*foommoh*]	noi avemmo [*ahvaymmoh*]
voi foste [*fosstay*]	voi aveste [*ahvaystay*]
essi furono [*foorohnoh*]	essi ebbero [*aybayroh*]
FUTURE	
io sarò [*sahroh*] **I shall be**	io avrò [*ahvroh*] **I shall have**
tu sarai [*sahrahee*]	tu avrai [*ahvrahee*]
egli sarà [*sahrah*]	egli avrà [*ahvrah*]
noi saremo [*sahraymoh*]	noi avremo [*ahvraymoh*]
voi sarete [*sahraytay*]	voi avrete [*ahvraytay*]
essi saranno [*sahrahnnoh*]	essi avranno [*ahvrahnnoh*]
CONDITIONAL	
io sarei [*sahrayee*] **I should be**	io avrei [*ahvrayee*] **I should have**
tu saresti [*sahresstee*]	tu avresti [*ahvresstee*]
egli sarebbe [*sahrebbay*]	egli avrebbe [*ahvrebbay*]
noi saremmo [*sahraymmoh*]	noi avremmo [*ahvraymmoh*]
voi sareste [*sahresstay*]	voi avreste [*ahvresstay*]
essi sarebbero [*sahrebbayroh*]	essi avrebbero [*ahvrebbayroh*]
IMPERATIVE	
sii [*seeee*] **be**	abbi [*ahbbee*] **have**
sia [*seeah*]	abbia [*ahbbyah*]
siamo [*seeahmoh*]	abbiamo [*ahbbyahmoh*]
siate [*seeahtay*]	abbiate [*ahbbyahtay*]
siano [*seeahnoh*]	abbiano [*ahbbyahnoh*]

PAST PERFECT

io ero stato **I had been**	io avevo avuto **I had had**
[ayroh stahtoh]	*[ahvayvoh ahvootoh]*
tu eri stato	tu avevi avuto
[ayree stahtoh]	*[ahvayvee ahvootoh]*
egli era stato	egli aveva avuto
[ayrah stahtoh]	*[ahvayvah ahvootoh]*
essa era stata	essa aveva avuto
[ayrah stahtah]	*[ahvayvah ahvootoh]*
noi eravamo stati	noi avevamo avuto
[ayrahvahmoh stahtee]	*[ahvayvahmoh ahvootoh]*
voi eravate state	voi avevate avuto
[ayrahvaytay stahtee]	*[ahvayvahtay ahvootoh]*
essi erano stati	essi avevano avuto
[ayrahnoh stahtee]	*[ahvayvahnoh ahvootoh]*
esse erano state	esse avevano avuto
[ayrahnoh stahtay]	*[ahvayvahnoh ahvootoh]*

INFINITIVE

essere *[esssayray]* **to be**	avere *[ahvayray]* **to have**

GERUND

essendo *[esssendoh]* **being**	avendo *[ahvendoh]* **having**

PAST PARTICIPLE

m. stato *[stahtoh]* **been**	*m.* avuto *[ahvootoh]* **had**
f. stata *[stahtah]*	*f.* avuta *[ahvootah]*
p.m. stati *[stahtee]*	*p.m.* avuti *[ahvootee]*
p.f. state *[stahtay]*	*p.f.* avute *[ahvootay]*

PRESENT PERFECT

io sono stato **I have been**	io ho avuto **I have had**
[sohnoh stahtoh]	*[oh ahvootoh]*
tu sei stato	tu hai avuto
[sayee stahtoh]	*[ahee ahvootoh]*
egli è stato	egli ha avuto
[ay stahtoh]	*[ah ahvootoh]*
essa è stata	essa ha avuto
[ay stahtah]	*[ah ahvootoh]*
noi siamo stati	noi abbiamo avuto
[seeahmoh stahtee]	*[ahbbyahmoh ahvootoh]*
voi siete stati	voi avete avuto
[seeaytay stahtee]	*[ahvaytay ahvootoh]*
essi sono stati	essi hanno avuto
[sohnoh stahtee]	*[ahnnoh ahvootoh]*
esse sono state	esse hanno avuto
[sohnoh stahtay]	*[ahnnoh ahvootoh]*

THE THREE CONJUGATIONS

There are 3 groups, or Conjugations of Italian verbs. The infinitives consist of a stem followed by the endings *-are*, *-ere* and *-ire*.

Ex:	mandare	credere	partire
	[*mahndāhray*]	[*crāydayray*]	[*pahrtēēray*]
	to send	**to believe**	**to leave**
		to think	**to start**

The indicative present is formed by adding the following terminations to the Stem:

Singular	1st Pers.	2nd Pers.	3rd Pers.
-are	-o	-i	-a
-ere	-o	-i	-e
-ire	-o	-i	-e
Plural	1st Pers.	2nd Pers.	3rd Pers.
-are	-iamo	-ate	-ano
-ere	-iamo	-ete	-ono
-ire	-iamo	-ite	-ono

Note that the terminations of the three Conjugations are alike in the 1st and 2nd Persons Singular, and 1st Person Plural, and that *-ere* and *-ire* Verbs only differ in the 2nd Person Plural.
It is to be remembered that the Nominative Pronoun is generally omitted in Italian, the verb ending usually being sufficient to indicate the person.

The full Conjugations are as follow:

I send	**I believe**	**I start**
io mando	io credo	io parto
[*māhndoh*]	[*krāydoh*]	[*pāhrtoh*]
tu mandi	tu credi	tu parti
[*māhndee*]	[*krāydee*]	[*pāhrtee*]
egli manda	egli crede	egli parte
[*māhndah*]	[*krāyday*]	[*pāhrtay*]
noi mandiamo	noi crediamo	noi partiamo
[*mahndeeāhmoh*]	[*kraydeeāhmoh*]	[*pahrteeāhmo*]
voi mandate	voi credete	voi partite
[*mahndāhtay*]	[*kraydāytay*]	[*pahrtēētay*]
essi mandano	essi credono	essi partono
[*māhndahnoh*]	[*krāydohnoh*]	[*pāhrtohnoh*]

THE IMPERFECT TENSE

The imperfect Tense is formed by taking away the final *re* or the Infinitive, and adding the following Terminations:

-vo -vi -va -vamo -vate -vano

The full Conjugations are therefore as follow:

I was sending	**I was believing**	**I was starting**
io mandavo [*mahndahvoh*]	io credevo [*kraydayvoh*]	io partivo [*pahrteevoh*]
tu mandavi [*mahndahvee*]	tu credevi [*kraydayvee*]	tu partivi [*pahrteevee*]
egli mandava [*mahndahvah*]	egli credeva [*kraydayvah*]	egli partiva [*pahrteevah*]
noi mandavamo [*mahndahvahmoh*]	noi credevamo [*kraydayvahmoh*]	noi partivamo [*pahrteevahmoh*]
voi mandavate [*mahndahvahtay*]	voi credevate [*kraydayvahtay*]	voi partivate [*pahrteevahtay*]
essi mandavano [*mahndahvahnoh*]	essi credevano [*kraydayvahnoh*]	essi partivano [*pahrteevahnoh*]

THE SIMPLE PAST

The Simple Past of Verbs ending in *-are* is formed by adding the following Terminations to the Stem:

-ai -asti -ò -ammo -aste -arono

-ere Verbs change the first Vowel of these Terminations to *e*; *-ire* Verbs change it to *i*. The full Conjugations are as follow:

I sent	**I believed**	**I started**
io mandai [*mahndahee*]	io credei [*kraydayee*]	io partii [*pahrteeee*]
tu mandasti [*mahndahstee*]	tu credesti [*kraydaystee*]	tu partisti [*pahrteestee*]
egli mandò [*mahndo*]	egli credè [*krayday*]	egli partì [*pahrtee*]
noi mandammo [*mahndahmmoh*]	noi credemmo [*kraydaymmoh*]	noi partimmo [*pahrteemmoh*]
voi mandaste [*mahndahstay*]	voi credeste [*kraydaystay*]	voi partiste [*pahrteestay*]
essi mandarono [*mahdahrohnoh*]	essi crederono [*kraydayrohnoh*]	essi partirono [*pahrteerohnoh*]

THE FUTURE TENSE

The Future Tense is formed by taking away the final *e* on the Infinitive, and adding the following Terminations:

Singular			*Plural*		
1st Pers.	2nd Pers.	3rd Pers.	1st Pers.	2nd Pers.	3rd Pers.
-ò	-ai	-à	-emo	-ete	-anno

Verbs ending in *-are* change the *a* into *e* in the Future Tense.
The full Conjugations are therefore as follow:

I shall send	**I shall believe**	**I shall start**
io manderò [*mahndayroh*]	io crederò [*kraydayroh*]	io partirò [*pahrteeroh*]
tu manderai [*mahndayrahee*]	tu crederai [*kraydayrahee*]	tu partirai [*pahrteerahee*]
egli manderà [*mahndayrah*]	egli crederà [*kraydayrah*]	egli partirà [*pahrteerah*]
noi manderemo [*mahndayraymoh*]	noi crederemo [*kraydayraymoh*]	noi partiremo [*pahrteeraymoh*]
voi manderete [*mahndayraytay*]	voi crederete [*kraydayraytay*]	voi partirete [*pahrteeraytay*]
essi manderanno [*mahndayrahnnoh*]	essi crederanno [*kraydayrahnnoh*]	essi partiranno [*pahrteerahnnoh*]

THE CONDITIONAL TENSE

The Conditional Tense is formed by taking off the final *o* from the 1st Person Singular of the Future Tense, and adding

-ei -esti -ebbe -emmo -este -ebbero

io manderei [*mahndayraye*] **I should send**
egli/ella crederebbe [*kraydayrebbay*] **he/she would believe**
essi/esse partirebbero [*pahrteeraybbayroh*] **they would start**

THE IMPERATIVE (First and Second Person Plural)

is the same as the Present Indicative, thus:

mandiamo **let us send** [*mahndeeahmoh*]
crediamo **let us believe** [*kraydeeahmoh*]
partiamo **let us start** [*pahrteeahmoh*]
non dormiamo **do not let us sleep** [*non dohrmeeahmoh*]

mandate **send** [*mahndahtay*]
credete **believe** [*kraydaytay*]
partite **start** [*pahrteetay*]
non dormite **do not sleep** [*non dohrmeetay*]

THE SUBJUNCTIVE

The Present Subjunctive is formed by adding the following Terminations to the Stem:

Verbs in *-are*: -i -i -i; -iamo -iate -ino
Verbs in *-ere*: -a -a -a; -iamo -iate -ano

Ex: mandi, mandi, mandi; mandiamo, mandiate, mandino;
parta, parta, parta; partiamo, partiate, partano

Verbs conjugated like capire add *isc*, as in the Present Indicative thus:

capisca, capisca, capisca; capiamo, capite, capiscano

The Imperfect Subjunctive of all Verbs (irregular included) is formed by taking off *sti* from the Second Person Singular of the Past Definite, and adding

-ssi -ssi -sse; -ssimo -ste -ssero

Ex: fumassi, fumassi, fumasse; fumassimo, fumaste, fumassero
finissi, finissi, finisse; finissimo, finiste, finissero

PRESENT AND PAST PARTICIPLES

are formed by adding the following Terminations to the Stem:

Verbs ending in *-are*	-ando	-ato
Verbs ending in *-ere*	-endo	-uto
Verbs ending in *-ire*	-endo	-ito

Ex: mandando **sending**	mandato **sent**
[*mahdāhndoh*]	[*mahndāhtoh*]
credendo **believing**	creduto **believed**
[*craydēndoh*]	[*craydōotoh*]
partendo **starting**	partito **started**
[*pahrtēndoh*]	[*pahrtēetoh*]

There is also a form of the Present Participle, ending in *te* instead of *do*. It is generally used as an adjective, thus:

un fanciullo dormiente — a sleeping child

The Present Participle is not much employed in Italian.

IRREGULAR VERBS

Semi-irregularities of some verbs in *-are*

1. Verbs ending in *-care* and *-gare*, as: pagare, to pay; cercare, to look for; pregare, to pray; mancare, to fail; giudicare, to judge, when the *c* or *g* is followed by *e* or *i*, take an *h* in order to preserve the hard sound of the consonant.

io pago	che io paghi
tu paghi	che tu paghi
egli paga	che egli paghi
noi paghiamo	che noi paghiamo
voi pagate	che voi paghiate
essi pagano	che essi paghino

2. In the Future they make pagherò, pregherò, cercherò, mancherò, etc.:

egli pagherà il suo conto	he will pay his bill
noi pregheremo per lei	we shall pray for her

3. Verbs in *-ciare* and in *-giare* or *-sciare* as: cominciare, to *begin*; lasciare, to leave; mangiare, to eat; drop the *i* before *e* or *i*

	io mangio	io comincio
	tu mangi	tu cominci
Fut.	mangerò	comincerò

4. Verbs in *-iare* having a stress on the *i*, as; spiare, to spy; inviare, to send; obliare, to forget, retain the *i*, even before the other *i* of the 2nd singular person of the Present Indicative

tu invii una lettera	you send a letter
noi non vi oblieremo	we shan't forget you

5. Verbs in *-chiare*, *-gliare*, and *-oiare*, as; pigliare, to take; invecchiare, to grow old; annoiare, to bore; drop the *i* when followed by another *i*:

	io piglio	io annoio
	tu pigli	tu annoi
Fut.	piglierò	annoierò

Peculiarities of some verbs in *-ere*

Some verbs of the 2nd conjugation have two distinct terminations for the 1st and 3rd person singular, and for the 3rd plural of the Simple Past

io credei	io credetti
tu credesti	
egli credè	egli credette
noi credemmo	
voi credeste	
essi crederono	essi credettero

Semi-irregulaties of some verbs in *-ire*

1. The verb cucire, to sew; and sdrucire, to rend, take an *i* whenever the *c* precedes an *a* or an *o*

io cucio	io sdrucio
tu cuci	tu sdruci
egli cuce	egli sdruce
noi cuciamo	noi sdruciamo
voi cucite	voi sdrucite
essi cuciono	essi sdruciono

2. A large number of the verbs in *-ire* in the 1st, 2nd, and 3rd sing., and in the 3rd plural of the Indicative, take the termination *isco*, *isci*, *isce*, *iscono*, instead of the regular forms. A similar change takes place in the Present Subjunctive and in the Imperative

I understand	**that I understand**
io capisco	ch'io capisca
tu capisci	che tu capisca
egli capisce	ch'egli capisca
noi capiamo	che noi capiamo
voi capite	che voi capiate
essi capiscono	ch'essi capiscano

3. The following verbs are conjugated like capire

finire **to finish**	costituire **to constitute**
preferire **to prefer**	digerire **to digest**
riverire **to revere**	esibire **to exhibit**
fiorire **to flourish**	suggerire **to suggest**
ferire **to wound**	abbellire **to beautify**
definire **to define**	appassire **to fade**
demolire **to demolish**	punire **to punish**
patire **to suffer**	ardire **to dare**
arrossire **to blush**	costruire **to construct**
restituire **to restore**	compatire **to pity**
ubbidire **to obey**	progredire **to progress**
colpire **to strike**	impallidire **to become pale**

THE NEGATIVE FORM

The Negative form of verbs is formed by putting non before the verb. Do, does and did are not translated.

Ex: non fumo	I do not smoke
non abbiamo i biglietti	we have not got the tickets.

THE INTERROGATIVE FORM

As the pronoun is usually omitted, questions are indicated by the tone of voice. Do, does and did are not translated.

Ex: capisci?	do you understand?
abbiamo tempo?	have we time?

COMPOUND TENSES

The verb essere is conjugated with itself

Ex: egli è stato — he has been (he is been)

All reflexive verbs and most intransitive ones are also conjugated with essere. The Past Participle following essere must always agree in number and gender with the subject.

REFLEXIVE VERBS

The reflexive pronouns come before the verb except in the Infinitive, the Present Participle and the Imperative (affermative not polite form) when they follow and are joined on to the verb.

Ex: alzarsi	to get up
alzandosi	getting up
alzati	get up

but,

io mi alzo	I get up
noi ci alziamo	we get up
essi si alzano	they get up

THE PROGRESSIVE FORM

This is used very little in Italian, the Present Indicative being used where in English we would adopt this form. When, however, it is important to indicate that the action in question was or is taking place at the moment referred to, the verb stare is used, and not essere, in progressive tenses.

Ex: Lo sta facendo adesso	He is doing it now
Non stava lavorando?	Wasn't he working?

The verb avere and not essere is used to form certain phrases where we use to be in English

aver caldo/freddo	to be hot, cold
aver fame/sete	to be hungry, thirsty
aver ragione/torto	to be right, wrong
aver 10 anni	to be 10 years old
aver paura	to be frightened
aver fretta	to be in a hurry
aver vergogna	to be ashamed
aver mal di mare	to be sea-sick

PREPOSITIONS

to-at	a	[*ah*]
of	di	[*dee*]
in	dentro, in	[*dentroh, een*]
on	su, sopra	[*soo, soprah*]
by, from	da	[*dah*]
with	con	[*kon*]
under	sotto	[*sottoh*]
before	prima di	[*preemah dee*]
after	dopo	[*dohpoh*]
until	fino a	[*feenoh ah*]
for	per	[*pehr*]
near	vicino a	[*veecheenoh ah*]
behind	dietro	[*deeaytroh*]

CONJUNCTIONS

and	e	[*short sound as in* '*egg*']
but	ma	[*mah*]
if	se	[*as in* '*sent*']
now	ora	[*ohrah*]
while	mentre	[*mentray*]
where	dove	[*dohvay*]
that	che	[*kay*]
either...or	o...o	[*as in* '*on*']
neither...nor	né...né	[*as in* '*neck*']
because / why	perché	[*pehrkay*]
as...as	così...come	[*kohzee komay*]
	tanto...quanto	[*tahntoh kwahntoh*]
as	come	[*komay*]

It will be seen that 'why' and 'because' are both translated by 'perché' in Italian.

INDEX

Finito di stampare nel febbraio 2002
dalle Industrie per le Arti Grafiche Garzanti-Verga s.r.l.
Cernusco sul Naviglio (Mi)

